£18.49

KT-489-658

Essentials of Marketing

Third edition

ESSENTIALS OF MARKETING

MARKETING

THE LEARNING CENTRE
TOWER HAMLETS COLLEGE
ARBOUR SQUARE
LONDON E1 0PS

THIRD EDITION

MICHAEL CANT

JUTA

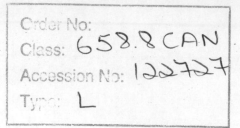
First published 1999
Second impression 2003
Second edition 2004
Third edition 2010

Juta & Company Ltd
1st floor, Sunclare Building, 21 Dreyer Street, Claremont 7708

© 2010 Juta & Company Ltd

ISBN: 978 –0–70217–769–9

Project manager: Marlinee Chetty
Copy editor: Wendy Priilaid
Indexer: Sanet Le Roux
Typesetter: ANdtp Services
Cover designer: Jacques Nel
Printed in South Africa by Mills Litho, Maitland, Cape Town

The authors and the publisher have made every effort to obtain permission for and to acknowledge the use of copyright material. Should any infringement of copyright have occurred, please contact the publisher, and every effort will be made to rectify omissions or errors in the event of a reprint or new edition.

Preface

Essentials of Marketing is designed to give students the opportunity to learn about marketing in an enjoyable and practical way. Marketing takes place all around us. Marketing is an essential service in all types of businesses, from manufacturing companies to wholesalers and retailers to service organisations.

It is fair to say that marketing is essential to all kinds of individuals and organisations. You will realise how widespread marketing is when it emerges that large retailers, doctors, lawyers, dentists, politicians and even churches use marketing techniques all the time.

It is therefore important that these organisations know what marketing is, what the marketing environment entails, how to research the market properly, which factors influence consumers' behaviour and how to segment the market. All these tasks are performed in order to satisfy the needs of the customers and to eventually influence a decision on what specific product(s) to offer, at what price, where the products should be offered and how the customers should be informed of the products.

Essentials of Marketing has been designed as a result of the developments in higher education. The current trend is towards the modular system of teaching as well as a focus on specialist degrees and diplomas. *Essentials of Marketing* has been structured to provide student marketers with a good foundation for the formulation of a marketing strategy. We believe that this book serves this purpose and that it is ideally suited for a modular course in marketing. The authors of the text are all specialists in their fields. The fact that the authors are all experienced writers of professional articles and academic texts, and have read many papers at international conferences, as well as having vast practical experience, ensures that this text achieves a good balance between the academic and practical approaches to marketing.

Care has been taken to present the content in a logical and systematic manner and this text has succeeded in achieveing this.

The following authors have been involved in the writing of this text:

- Chapter 1 – Prof Michael Cant (Unisa)
- Chapter 2 – Prof Johan Strydom (Unisa)
- Chapter 3 – Prof Annekie Brink (Unisa)
- Chapter 4 – Prof Chris Jooste (RAU)
- Chapter 5 – Prof Michael Cant (Unisa)
- Chapter 6 – Mr Ricardo Machado (Unisa)
- Chapter 7 – Prof Michael Cant (Unisa)

We trust that you will enjoy using *Essentials of Marketing* and that you will benefit from the content.

MC Cant

January 2010

Contents

CHAPTER ONE

The field of marketing

Learning objectives

After you have studied this chapter you will be able to:

- explain what marketing is;
- explain the concept of exchange;
- describe the marketing activities;
- discuss the four main marketing orientations;
- define marketing;
- explain the marketing process; and
- discuss the marketing function in an organisation.

1.1 Introduction[1]

Marketing is a fundamental part of our daily lives. About half of every rand spent pays for marketing costs, such as marketing research, product development, packaging, transportation, storage, advertising and sales expenses. By developing a better understanding of marketing, you will become a better-informed consumer. You will better understand the buying process and be able to negotiate more effectively with sellers. Moreover, you will be better prepared to demand satisfaction when the goods and services you buy do not meet the standards promised by the manufacturer or the marketer.

The ultimate goal of all marketing activity is to facilitate *mutually satisfying exchanges between parties.* The activities of marketing include the *conception, pricing, promotion* and *distribution* of ideas, products and services.

The role of marketing and the character of marketing activities within an organisation are strongly influenced by its philosophy and orientation. A *production-oriented* organisation focuses on the internal capabilities of the company rather than on the desires and needs of the marketplace. A *sales-oriented* organisation is based on the beliefs that people will buy more products if aggressive sales techniques are used, and that high sales volumes produce high profits. A *marketing-oriented* organisation focuses on satisfying customer wants and needs while meeting company objectives. A *societal marketing-oriented* organisation goes beyond a pure marketing orientation to include the preservation or enhancement of individuals' and society's long-term best interests.

In order for the marketing concept to be fully implemented throughout the organisation, management must enthusiastically embrace and endorse the concept, and encourage its use in every department. Changing from a production or sales orientation to a marketing orientation often requires changes in authority and responsibility for management.

The marketing process includes understanding the organisation's mission and the role that marketing plays in fulfilling it, setting marketing objectives, scanning the environment, developing a marketing strategy by selecting a target market strategy, developing and implementing a marketing mix, implementing the strategy, designing performance measures, evaluating marketing efforts and making changes if needed. The marketing mix combines product, distribution (place), marketing communication and pricing strategies in a way that creates exchanges satisfying to both individual and company objectives.

We also discuss strategic marketing management. Synergy must be obtained and all four marketing instruments (i.e. product, place, promotion and price) combined into a strategy where strategic decisions will support and reinforce each other. Marketing strategies such as competitive, growth and survival strategies are discussed as viable strategic options. Strategic decisions are taken at top-management level and usually also entail close cooperation between marketing and the various functional departments. Planning the market and marketing strategies of a company with several business units is much more complicated than planning the implementation of a single integrated marketing strategy.

All these aspects are discussed in this chapter.

1.2 The nature of marketing

1.2.1 Marketing[2]

The term marketing is a very broad concept and means many things to many people. Some people see marketing merely as selling something, some see it as advertisements aimed at selling something, some see it as the movement of products from where they are manufactured to where they are consumed, while others see it only as the retail outlet where products are bought. Everyone is right to some degree, as marketing includes all of these things and more.

Marketing actually has two sides. On one side it is a management orientation which is focused on customers – that is, to satisfy their needs. On the other side, it is a number of activities that are combined in such a way so that not only are customers' needs met but a profit is also made. The American Marketing Association's definition includes both these aspects: 'Marketing is the process of planning and executing the conception, pricing, marketing communication and distribution of ideas, products, and services to create exchanges that satisfy individual and organisational goals.' These all refer to specific decision-making areas of marketing management.

The challenges posed by the new millennium are vastly different from those of the past, and therefore marketing cannot be defined as just 'making a sale', but rather the identifying and understanding of customers' needs, and the satisfaction of these needs. If the marketer understands the basic activities of marketing – which include understanding consumer needs, developing products that provide superior value – price that product correctly, and distribute and promote it effectively, the chances of product success are much higher. Marketing thus encompasses a 'set of processes for creating, communicating, and delivering value to customers' in a mutually beneficial relationship between the organisation and all its relevant stakeholders (American Marketing Association, 2005).[3]

Experian – entering a new market with a new product

Experian is a credit reference agency. It holds details on consumers' credit ratings and makes them available to businesses such as banks and credit card issuers who need such information. Consumers need this service to be able to check that their credit details are accurate. The new product allows consumers to monitor creditworthiness online and, in particular, helps to check that they have not been victims of identity fraud. This is a serious problem in the UK, involving a criminal applying for credit in someone else's name. Igor Ansoff, a business expert, showed the ways in which businesses can expand on a grid. They could develop:

- Existing products in existing markets. This is called market penetration and involves increasing the market share of the business.
- New products in an existing market. This is called product development. In Experian's case this would involve expanding their business-to-business products.
- Existing products in new markets. This is called market development.

Experian has expanded into over 60 countries worldwide new products in new markets. This is called diversification. CreditExpert is an example. This is the highest risk strategy needing new skills and technique.

Source: Anon, 2008. *Entering a new market with a new product.* [Online] Available from: http://www.times100.co.uk/ (accessed: 14 July 2008).[4]

As marketing deals with the offering of products or services, it implies that there are exchanges that need to take place – that is, between the place of production and the place of consumption.

1.2.2   Exchange and marketing

Central to the marketing process is *exchange*. Exchange in essence means that people are prepared to offer something up in order to receive something in return – that is, something that will satisfy their needs.

In our everyday lives we generally associate money as the means by which we perform this exchange as we hand over money (pay) to the seller in return for the goods or service we require. Exchange does not necessarily require money, however.[5] Two persons may, for example, exchange books, or swap a vehicle for a timeshare unit, and so forth.

Lamb et al indicate that five conditions must prevail for any kind of exchange to take place:[6]

- There must be at least two parties.
- Each party must have something that the other party values.
- Each party must be able to communicate with the other party, and deliver the goods or services sought by the other party.
- Each party must be free to accept or reject the other's offer.
- Each party must want to deal with the other party.

A market exists if the previous conditions prevail, but that does not imply that an exchange will actually take place between the parties. These conditions are, however, required for an exchange to happen. Take, for example, a person listing a flat for sale with an estate agent for R500 000. A number of people may be brought to the flat by the agent and some offers may even be made, but unless the seller accepts an offer, no exchange will take place.[7]

When exchange takes place, certain gaps are created between production and consumption. These gaps are discussed in the next section.

1.2.3 Gaps between production and consumption

The place where a product is produced is not necessarily the place where it is consumed and this causes gaps in the marketing process. Identifying these gaps can be described as *core marketing aspects*.

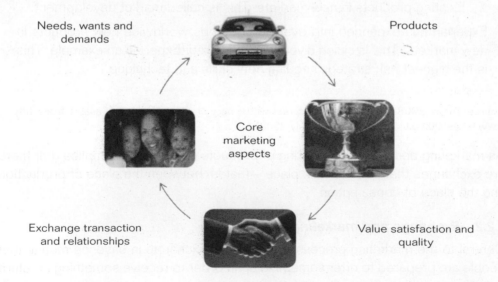

Needs, wants and demands

Products

Core marketing aspects

Exchange transaction and relationships

Value satisfaction and quality

Figure 1.1 The core marketing aspects
Source: Adapted from Kotler, P & Armstrong, G. 2006. *Principles of marketing*, 7th ed. Englewood Cliffs, NJ: Prentice Hall, Inc, p 6.

Figure 1.1 shows that the core marketing aspects are linked, with each aspect building on the one before it.

Various gaps can be identified between these core aspects. For instance, a consumer who wants to buy a new car must be able to have options of colour, brand, etc. For this an exchange – money – takes place. The gaps that can be identified here lie in the transport of the product, availability in colour range, engine size, etc.

The successful marketing of a suitable market offering is possible only if all the gaps in the process have been effectively bridged. According to McInnis,[8] five types of gaps can be distinguished:

- *Space gap.* Amalgamated Beverage Industries (ABI), the large company that bottles various soft drinks and other products such as Coca-Cola in South Africa, needs ways to distribute its products throughout South Africa because there is a geographical space (distance) between the manufacturer and the consumer.
- *Time gap.* As various vegetables and fruits that can only be grown and harvested in the summer are sought after the whole year round, distributors have to store large numbers for distribution throughout the year.
- *Information gap.* Medicine is a sensitive consumer product because it affects the consumer in a very personal manner. However, few consumers are informed enough to know which medicine to use with a particular ailment, hence the need for advertisements and pharmacists who can inform consumers in this respect.
- *Ownership gap.* When a new house is purchased, the consumer becomes the owner only when it is registered in his or her name. However, the consumer requires finance from a bank to make the purchase possible.
- *Value gap.* Both the seller and the buyer must agree on an acceptable exchange rate (price of the product). If the buyer regards a price of R200 for a pair of jeans as acceptable, he or she will purchase the jeans. This means that the value the buyer attaches to the product is the same as that attached by the seller.

Over the years the gaps between the buyer and seller resulted in the development of an acceptable form of exchange which represented the perceived value (or price) of those products they wanted to exchange. This enabled the parties to exchange products not only for other products but also for the acceptable form of exchange (such as pieces of silver or gold, or emeralds).

Today media that are used for exchange purposes are many and varied. There are paper notes, coins, credit and debit cards, eBucks, and so forth.

Transporting products and conveying information have become increasingly complicated over time, creating an opportunity for the specialised services of intermediaries, who bridge the gap between buyer and seller and act as go-betweens for participants who are no longer in close contact. They are paid for their efforts by means of an acceptable exchange medium.

There are three main kinds of intermediaries:

- *Middlemen* are directly involved in taking title of products which are later sold to others. The first middlemen were probably hawkers who traded in a variety of products and also conveyed vital information about potential markets and desirable new products. They later made way for large wholesalers and retailers to facilitate exchanges between buyers and sellers. Pep Stores, for example, is an enterprise which is a middleman for a wide variety of products offered to customers under the same roof.
- *Sales intermediaries* are agents who do not take title of products they sell. They provide and are paid for services to facilitate the sales process.
- *Auxiliary enterprises* are not directly involved in the transfer of title but provide support services to facilitate the selling process. Examples are Transnet, advertising agencies and commercial banks.

Vodacom puts users on the map

In a first for South African cellphone users, Vodacom launched two innovative personal social networking services.

The services, Meep – a real-time, presence-based instant messaging service – and TheGRID will allow South Africans to enter the location-based social networking space from their cellphones.

Source: Fin24, 2007.

Without modern society's desire for new and enjoyable things, stagnation and decline are inevitable. Such desires play a crucial role in economic development. There is a large market consisting of people with a wide variety of needs, which creates a demand for all kinds of need-satisfying products and services. Sellers try to fulfil these needs in order to satisfy their own, which include a profit objective.

Price reflects the value of that specific product to the buyer. The perceived 'price' of a product is not only its monetary value, but also includes factors such as the time cost (the amount of money that could have been generated in the time spent to attain the product) and emotional cost (the emotional exertion the consumer had to go through to obtain the product, for example anger towards an unprofessional shop assistant) among others. Today consumers do not simply buy a physical object; they buy a market offering which combines the physical object with other need-satisfying qualities

The filling of the gaps, as identified earlier, necessitates the performance of certain actions or activities.

1.3 Marketing activities

Marketing activities can be defined as those activities used to transfer the market offering to the buyer. The following primary, auxiliary and exchange activities can be distinguished.[9]

The *primary marketing activity* is *transport*. From donkeys and camels, transport methods have evolved to include pipelines, and land, water and air traffic, each with its own unique advantages and disadvantages. The purpose of these forms of transport is to deliver the product to the consumer in the quickest and safest way.

The *auxiliary marketing activities* include the following:

- *Sourcing and supplying information.* The seller must know who and where potential buyers are. This information can be obtained by conducting marketing research. Thereafter the seller can supply information to potential buyers by using marketing communication methods such as advertising and personal selling.
- *Standardisation and grading.* In order to close the gap between seller and buyer, manufactured products must be designed to conform to specific norms or standards. Agricultural products are graded according to certain qualities. Eggs, for example, are graded according to size. The John Platter Wine Guide is the grading system for wine where one to five stars are awarded to wines of similar quality. This facilitates the buying process, making it easier for the buyer to distinguish between the ever-increasing varieties of products available.
- *Storage.* This is an activity that closes the time gap. The seasonal production of agricultural products necessitates storage to ensure an even consumption of these products throughout the year. Warehouses are normally used for storage. For example, mealies are stored in silos from where they are delivered to milling companies as needed for distribution to wholesalers and retailers.
- *Financing.* Costs which are incurred in the transfer of products and services from sellers to buyers must be financed – usually by banks and other financial institutions. All the participants in the exchange process should strive to keep financing costs down so that the product can be presented to the consumer at a viable price.
- *Risk taking.* The owner of the product is exposed to certain risks, such as arson or theft, and can take out insurance as a form of protection against them.

The *exchange marketing activities* are *buying* and *selling*. Ownership is transferred from one person to the other. Buying activities are not regarded as a marketing task but rather as the responsibility of the purchasing department. Selling, on the other hand, is a very important task of the marketing department of any organisation. Over the years these marketing activities have, however, been influenced by the prevailing marketing orientation of the time.

1.4 Marketing orientations[10]

An organisation's marketing activities are strongly influenced by the organisation's marketing orientation. Four main competing orientations have influenced organisations over the years. These are commonly referred to as production, sales, marketing and societal marketing orientations, and each is briefly discussed below.

1.4.1 Production orientation

A production orientation is largely focused on the internal capabilities of a company instead of on the needs of the market. This in fact means that the management assesses its own resources and asks questions such as: 'What are we good at?'; 'What are our fields of expertise?'; 'Is there anything we can manufacture well and cost effectively?'. In a similar way, service organisations will evaluate their position and ask similar questions.[11] The *internal capability of the organisation* is therefore the main focus point of the organisation, rather than the desires and needs of the marketplace.

This orientation's major shortfall lies in the fact that it does not consider whether the goods and services that the organisation produces most efficiently also meet the needs of the marketplace.

1.4.2 Sales orientation[12]

A sales orientation, still followed by many companies today, focuses on aggressive sales techniques to entice people or companies to buy their products. They also believe that high sales result in high profits. Not only is the focus on sales to the end user, but intermediaries such as retailers and wholesalers are also pressured into marketing the products aggressively. To sales-oriented organisations, marketing and selling can be regarded as synonymous.

An example of a strong sales-oriented approach is found in sales of timeshare. This approach in the industry gave it a bad reputation because some sales personnel do not allow consumers enough time to make responsible decisions. In fact many of these salespeople are trained in communication and persuasion skills in order to get people to make hasty and sometimes impulsive decisions. The emphasis is mostly on pressure selling. After the order has been signed it is regarded as a contract and the customer is compelled to pay, even if it is to his or her detriment. To avoid this, a 'cooling down' period has been instituted by government in some contracts (e.g. buying a house, timeshare, insurance). During this period (e.g. two days) the customer may cancel the contract if he or she so wishes without incurring any penalties.

The major shortcoming of a sales orientation is a lack of understanding of the needs and wants of the marketplace.

1.4.3 Marketing orientation (pure marketing concept)

After World War II, a shift in management's approach to the market occurred by way of a change from sales-oriented to marketing-oriented management, which resulted in an emphasis not only on the sales message and the price but also on the quality of products, the packaging thereof, the methods of distribution and the necessity to provide information by means of advertising.

A change in consumers' needs also took place in that they now had more sophisticated needs and were financially in a better position to satisfy them. Because consumers could now also choose from a wide variety of competing products, management realised the importance of the marketing function.

A marketing orientation is based on an understanding that a sale depends not on an aggressive sales force, but rather on a customer's decision to purchase a product. Perceived value also determines a business's products and its potential to prosper. To marketing-oriented firms, marketing means building long-term relationships with customers.[13]

This orientation has led to what is commonly called the *pure marketing concept*. This can be regarded as *an ethical code or philosophy according to which the marketing task is performed*. Many authors agree that the marketing concept serves as a guideline for management decision making.

The essence of the marketing concept lies in three principles, namely:

- consumer orientation;
- long-term maximisation of profitability; and
- the integration of all business activities directed at profitability and the satisfaction of consumer needs, demands and preferences.

1.4.3.1 Consumer orientation

The emphasis on consumers in marketing indicates that all marketing actions should be aimed at satisfying consumer needs, demands and preferences. This, however, does not mean that marketing management must provide for unrealistic consumer needs. The organisation can provide need satisfaction only insofar as its resources enable it to do so. Achieving the profitability objective must also be taken into account in the endeavour to provide for consumer needs. However, failure to appreciate what the consumer wants creates opportunities for competitors and can adversely affect profits.

There has been a change taking place in how organisations are being valued. Where traditionally organisations were measured by profit, and public companies by market capitalisation, these measures have given little indication of their future value.[14] Organisations are beginning to include additional measures by taking into account the value of the customer base.[15] Maximising the lifetime value of a customer is fundamental to relationship marketing.[16]

1.4.3.2 Profit orientation

Without profit, no company will be able to continue in its day-to-day operations for very long, thus, in the free-market system, achieving profitability is of crucial importance. Maximising profitability is the *primary objective* of a profit-seeking enterprise and can be achieved only with due consideration of consumer needs. The American Marketing Association describes an objective as 'the desired or needed result to be achieved by a specific time... [and] serve to provide guidance, motivation, evaluation and control.'[17]

The overriding profit objective of a company is usually expressed in quantitative terms. Profit-seeking organisations attempt to achieve a specific rate of return on total assets in the long term, rather than to obtain unduly high returns in the short term, as a short-term approach can endanger their survival. The long-term nature of the profitability objective distinguishes marketing from the bartering transaction from which it originally developed.

Non-profit-seeking organisations focus on effective and efficient utilisation of resources and cost reduction rather than on profits. In an economic decline, a profit-seeking organisation can also concentrate on efficiency and effectiveness rather than on profits in order to protect its position until economic conditions improve and profits can once again be made.

Secondary objectives are set in order to contribute directly – or even indirectly – to the achievement of the main objective.

- A secondary objective, for example, can be to enhance the corporate image of the organisation in the eyes of the public. Achievement of this objective can contribute indirectly to profitability.
- A secondary objective of increasing sales can influence the profit figure directly by increasing the income of the organisation.
- A secondary objective of promoting awareness of costs in the marketing department can have a direct influence on profit by encouraging cost reduction.
- Innovation can also be added to the list of secondary objectives in that companies that do not stay on the forefront of technological development will inevitably fall behind their competitors.

1.4.3.3 Organisational integration

The saying 'the sum of all the parts is greater than the whole' describes the basic principle of an organisational integration. A system is an integrated whole – a group of related units that work together to achieve a joint objective. This principle of the marketing concept is known as *organisational integration*. All departments in the organisation must work together to achieve the successful marketing of the organisation's market offering. All the divisions in the marketing department also direct their activities and decisions towards achieving a specific objective. Organisational integration goes hand in hand with the terms *synergy* and *total quality management* (TQM), which are discussed in section 1.5.2. Synergy between all the departments in an organisation can be achieved by adapting an attitude of quality deliverance to all the operations in an organisation whether it be production or sales. These three principles constitute the pure marketing concept.

The so-called pure marketing concept has been severely criticised as being shortsighted. A fourth principle was added to this concept, and today it includes the previous three principles (customer orientation, long-term maximisation of profitability and the integration of all activities) as well as *social responsibility*. This principle maintains that businesses are part of the larger society in which they operate, and are accountable to society for their performance. There should therefore be a balance between the needs of the customer, the profit the company wishes to make, its own integrated activities and the long-term best interests of society. The involvement of companies in community projects such as development of infrastructure, HIV/AIDS education and so forth are examples of social responsibility.

1.5 Relationship marketing[18]

1.5.1 A broader view of the market

Relationship marketing is a logical development in the gradual evolution of marketing thought. Relationship marketing places its main focus on the maintenance of long-term relationships between the organisation, the government, the public, the suppliers of raw materials, the employees, and current and potential consumers.

All the efforts of an organisation should be geared towards building these relationships. This is crucial for survival and growth, especially in an economic decline and in order to protect the competitive position.

Relationship marketing represents a broader view of the market and the marketing task, and evolved because of consumers' need for honest and open communication from management, and not only lip service to the marketing concept.

1.5.2 Expansion of the market offering

Relationship marketing acknowledges that different marketing strategies must be used for consumer acquisition and retention.[19] Relationship marketing implies that the four marketing instruments of product, place, promotion and price alone are inadequate to ensure full consumer satisfaction. The authors therefore conclude that two further variables must be added, namely *people* and *processes*. (See section 1.6.)

The *people* are the employees who should be well trained in customer service, and made to realise that their own job satisfaction ultimately rests on the success of the organisation in the market. *Processes* are integral parts of the production, administration and marketing functions.

Synergy means that the whole is more than the sum of its parts. When all the variables support each other, they reinforce the quality image of the product. The *total quality management* (TQM) principle, which in theory strives towards consumer satisfaction, underlies relationship marketing. However, this can only be an ideal of perfection and is closely related to the corporate culture where everybody must make an effort to realise this ideal.

1.5.3 A bigger market

Relationship marketing also entails a wider view of the market itself.

In the total market there are various smaller groupings, all with a greater or lesser influence on the marketing effort. Close relationships, especially with the important groupings, must be maintained.

Even though relationship marketing implies a wider view of the market, it also implores companies to adapt to an individual customer approach once the exact market as mentioned above has been finalised. According to Du Plessis, Jooste and Strydom,[20] relationship marketing differs from traditional segment-based marketing in that it endeavours to build a sustainable relationship with each and every one of its consumers to ensure repeat purchases.

Organisations are adopting *micro-segmentation* because of three important changes that have occurred that have rendered traditional segment-based marketing inappropriate:

- Consumers are more sophisticated and knowledgeable, which means that their expectations are rising.
- There have been drastic changes in technology.
- There has been an increase in competing vendors and products.

A change in company focus is evident in the explosion of the recent trend to market for a segment of one consumer. One example is the use of a *mass customisation* approach by companies who cater for the individual needs of consumers through the use of new technology.

Handling customer complaints is an important facet of an internal marketing programme, and well-founded complaints must receive immediate attention. The best and cheapest solution is to ensure that there are no complaints. It is important for companies to research the reasons for complaints. There must be ample opportunities for customers to direct complaints to responsible people who are able to take appropriate corrective action and in so doing prevent the loss of customers. Some car manufacturers, for example, have a customer care number with a direct line to the managing director. Consumers who are reluctant to complain but tend rather to avoid the unsatisfactory product or the situation in future are a grave threat to successful marketing. Consumers who are unhappy and who receive no satisfaction can also direct their complaints to the many consumer-action programmes (e.g. Wendy Knowler's consumer watch column in the *Cape Argus*) in the mass media, thereby causing unwelcome negative publicity for the organisation.

> **Examples of poor customer service**
> - Sales personnel chatting to each other while customers are waiting.
> - Sales personnel being disinterested or condescending, or those who make the customer feel unwelcome in any way.
> - Employees who are careless or incompetent.
> - Promises and/or delivery dates not kept.
> - Inadequate or incorrect information in advertising messages.
> - Receptionists who are unwilling or unable to handle telephone enquiries.

Some of the groups that can be identified are the following:[20]

- Current customers, whose loyalty is crucially important.
- Potential customers in unexploited markets, who must be contacted.
- Suppliers, who must be made aware of the importance of their cooperation in order to fully satisfy the needs of consumers. Suppliers contribute by timely delivery of quality raw materials, components and services. The excuse for bad customer service is so often that the spare parts/stock needed have not yet arrived, ignoring customer convenience.
- Potential employees, who must be carefully selected according to their abilities and especially their attitude towards customer service. Good employees prefer to work for successful companies.
- Reference groups who can convey the marketing message by direct personal contact ('word-of-mouth advertising'). The advantages of brand-loyal consumers, who not only repeatedly purchase the product but who also advise friends to do so, can never be underestimated.
- The influencers such as government, who may be able to exert an influence on the marketing activities of the business.
- Current employees, who are part of the internal market. Management has a responsibility to train, motivate and remunerate employees but must, furthermore, also persuade these employees to actively support marketing decisions and strategies.

Relationship marketing is in fact the essence of a market-driven approach to marketing management.

1.6 Defining marketing[21]

It is imperative to first have a good understanding of the nature and extent of the marketing process before one can clearly define marketing. While it is true that no two authors agree on the exact formulation of a good definition of this complicated process, the following one best serves our purposes:

Marketing is the process of planning and executing the conception, pricing, promotion and distribution of ideas, goods and services to create exchanges that satisfy individual and organisational goals. Marketing is thus:

- about anticipating and satisfying consumer needs,
- by means of mutually beneficial exchange process, and
- doing so profitably and more effectively than competitors, by means of efficient managerial processes.[22]

1.7 The marketing process[23]

The four variables, known as the four Ps, about which the marketing management team has to take decisions are the *product* itself, the *place* where it is to be sold (distribution of the product), the marketing communication methods or *promotion* to be used to inform the consumer, and the *price* of the product which should reflect its value to the consumer. The four variables combine in a market offering which the consumer may decide to buy if it provides satisfaction of his or her needs. These four variables are known as the *marketing instruments* or as the *marketing mix*. Decisions regarding the four marketing instruments combine to form an integrated *marketing strategy* (or marketing plan), which is directed at a group of consumers in a specific environment for a specific market offering.

The larger the company's target market, usually the more advantageous it is for the manufacturer and the intermediaries. In the total consumer market there are many different groups. The members of each of these groups (also called *market segments*) have more or less similar characteristics, needs and product preferences. After careful consideration, marketing management selects from many different market segments a specific *target market* (or markets). The market offering is often changed in some way or another to meet the preferences of different target markets. It seldom happens that an organisation has only one single target market. Recent trends in marketing have introduced new concepts such as mass customisation, e-marketing and e-tailing, which imply that the Internet can be used to develop a marketing strategy for a single consumer, or in other words, markets of one.

There are usually also a number of competitors marketing similar products and competing for the patronage of the same target markets. Market offerings often differ only slightly from one another, perhaps only in the fact that they have different brand names. Consumers select – and purchase repeatedly – those brand names that afford them the greatest need satisfaction in terms of the sacrifice that they must make. Often, the sacrifice is not only in monetary terms – sometimes consumers are also willing to suffer some degree of inconvenience to obtain the desired brand-name product.

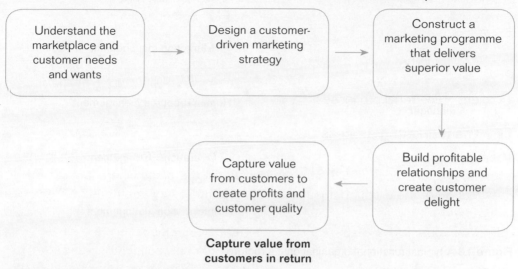

Create value for customers and build customer relationships

Understand the marketplace and customer needs and wants → Design a customer-driven marketing strategy → Construct a marketing programme that delivers superior value

Capture value from customers to create profits and customer quality ← Build profitable relationships and create customer delight

Capture value from customers in return

Figure 1.2 The marketing process

Source: Kotler, P & Armstrong, G. 2006. *Principles of marketing*, 11th ed. Englewood Cliffs, NJ: Prentice Hall, Inc, p 5.

1.8   The marketing function in the organisation

1.8.1   *The place of the marketing function*

At least seven different functional departments can be identified in today's large organisations of which the marketing function can be regarded as a key one due to its contribution to profits and its closeness to the consumer. The managers heading these seven departments must work together to realise the organisation's objectives and goals. A typical functional organisational structure is shown in figure 1.3.

The functions of these departments are described as follows:

- The *operations* function comprises the physical utilisation of raw materials and their conversion into manufactured materials and finished products, and is usually performed in a factory.
- The *human resource* function pertains to the acquisition, training, utilisation and retaining of a sufficient number of competent personnel.
- The *financial* function includes the acquisition, utilisation and control of the funds necessary for running the business. The main activities here are the acquisition and application of funds for the profitability, liquidity, solvency and continuity of the organisation.

Figure 1.3 A typical functional organisational structure

- The *purchasing* function ensures that the materials necessary for production are bought at the right places, at the right times, in the right quantities and at the right prices.
- The *public relations* function maintains and cultivates a favourable and objective image of the organisation among those whose opinion is important to the achievement of the business objectives.
- The *information* function makes available internal information for planning and control.
- The *marketing* function generates income from sales and is responsible for managing the marketing process.
- *General management* includes the activities of persons in managerial positions. These persons in top, middle and lower management have to plan for, organise, lead and control the organisation as a whole, as well as its individual functions. The general manager is at the head of the management team.

In practice there are also other functions and structures, and indeed other names may be used. It is important, however, to realise that the tasks of the different functional departments must be performed in both large and small organisations. The resources (capital) and abilities of various functionaries determine the existence and size of formal departments.

> The owner of a small business manufacturing and marketing children's clothing with the help of only a few machine operators has but one other manager who is responsible for both the production and the human resource functions. The owner herself acts as general and purchasing manager and is also responsible for the financial and marketing functions, of which public relations forms a part.

In very large multi-product organisations there can be even more different divisions than those shown in figure 1.3. There can be, for example, a marketing director directing several marketing managers for different products or product ranges. The marketing director provides leadership, and coordinates the activities of several different marketing departments. There are also many different organisational structures that can be identified of which the functional structure is only one example. Examples of different organisational structures include the matrix structures and line and staff structures, to name but a few.

What does a manager do? The workers tend to think that managers spend their working hours sitting and talking while there is real work to be done! However, there are three management tasks which must be performed by the management team. More about these tasks is provided in the section that follows.

1.8.2 The management tasks in marketing

The American Marketing Association describes marketing management as 'the process of setting marketing goals for an organisation (considering internal resources and market opportunities), the planning and execution of activities to meet these goals, and measuring progress toward their achievement'. They also note that this is an ongoing and repetitive process within the planning cycle to enable an organisation to continuously adapt to internal and external changes in the its environment.[24] These changes continuously create new problems and new opportunities. Thus, with effective management an organisation can stay ahead of competition by using changes in the environment to its advantage.

The management task consists, therefore, of a continuous process of planning, organising, leading and controlling marketing activities. Marketing management:

- identifies opportunities and threats in the marketing environment;
- identifies those opportunities which can be utilised in terms of internal strengths and weaknesses;
- compiles marketing data;
- chooses a specific target market;
- decides on the products to be produced in order to satisfy consumer needs;
- decides on the selling price of the products in order to attain the objective of profitability;
- decides on specific distribution channels;
- decides on marketing communication methods whereby consumers are informed, reminded and persuaded;
- decides on selection, training, remuneration and motivation of marketing personnel;
- organises and leads the activities of the marketing department; and
- controls the marketing process.

These responsibilities are part of the three management tasks, which are summarised in figure 1.4 and discussed below.

PLANNING

| Identify opportunities and threats | Set efficient global management schemes for corporate objectives | Decide on the marketing instruments and secure human resources |

IMPLEMENTATION

| Organise and coordinate the activities in the marketing department | Provide leadership in the planning and implementation of marketing strategies |

CONTROL/EVALUATION

Set standards and measure performance

Figure 1.4 The management task of marketing management

Source: Adapted from Van der Walt, A, Strydom, JW, Marx, S & Jooste, CJ. 1996. *Marketing management*, 3rd ed. Cape Town: Juta, p 14 and http://www.takeda.com/investor-information/management-tasks/article_933.html - 20k. 2008.

1.8.2.1 Planning

Planning by marketing management entails the examination of and the choice between various ways of utilising marketing opportunities, countering marketing threats and achieving marketing objectives. *Adaptive planning* is a framework for organising information, analysis, issues and opinions that form part of strategic decision making. A situation assessment is done to identify the internal and external factors impacting the organisation, as well as its past performance concerning these factors. Creative and strategic solutions are then conceptualised to address these factors. Marketing decisions thus begin with the identification and evaluation of marketing opportunities and threats, and internal strengths and weaknesses.

Contingency planning is another subdivision of planning that entails developing plans to provide an alternative to the main plan in the event that an unlikely but possible, external factor impacts on the original plan. It is the 'what will we do if ...' of planning. The contingency plan 'deals not with unforeseen events, but with events that were foreseen but considered unlikely to occur'.[25] For example, caterers always cater for more people than were specified in case more people show up than were planned for, or a waiter drops a plate while serving, or countless other scenarios.

1.8.2.2 Implementation

Organising and coordinating calls for the creation of an organisational structure best suited to the implementation of the marketing decisions in order to achieve marketing objectives. Marketing activities are grouped rationally, and individual divisions and managers are tasked with carrying them out. Finally, the levolo of authority, areao of responsibility, lines of communication and methods of co-ordination between the divisions and individuals are determined. Cooperation is achieved by integrating the interests of divisions, individuals, consumers, investors, suppliers and the community as a whole.

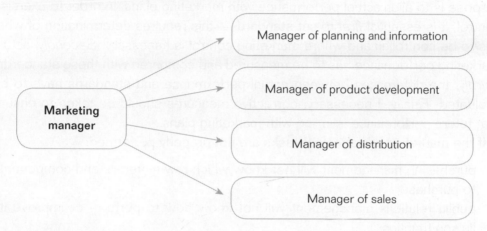

Figure 1.5 Functional organisational structure

Figure 1.5 shows a typical organisation chart of the different divisions in the marketing department under thc leadership of the marketing manager.

Leading involves a wide range of tasks, such as staffing, communicating and motivating. From a marketing viewpoint, leading embraces all the marketing decisions for putting preparation (planning, organising, coordinating, controlling) into practice. Briefly, once the marketing strategy has been formulated, people have to be found to perform the required marketing activities (staffing); they have to be instructed as to what they should do and told how well they are doing it (communicating); and a positive attitude towards work and the organisation must be carefully cultivated and maintained (motivating). Leading is therefore of paramount importance in the effective performance of the other management tasks.

Over time a few contemporary leadership styles have emerged including the following:[26]

- *Contingent reward leadership* is a leadership style where management closely supervises the employees, and facilitates all their activities and tasks.
- *Laissez faire leadership* is the opposite of contingent reward leadership in that management is minimally involved in the daily activities of personnel, leaving personnel to resort to their own devices.

- *Management-by-exception leadership* is a leadership style where managers intervene only when personnel's performance standards have not been met.
- In *transformational leadership*, leaders use inspiration and charisma, seeking to intellectually stimulate the sales personnel, and treat each employee as an individual. The ultimate goal of transformational leadership is to move personnel beyond their own self-interests toward those of the organisation.

1.8.2.3 Control

Controlling or evaluation is the regulatory task of marketing management, and its purpose is to align actual performance with marketing plans. In order to exercise control, it is essential *first* to set standards – this requires determination of what has to be controlled and where marketing control is necessary. *Secondly*, actual marketing performance has to be measured and compared with these standards. *Thirdly*, the differences between actual performance and standards have to be evaluated. *Finally*, if necessary, corrective measures should be taken to ensure that future performance is in line with marketing plans.

If the marketing management tasks are not properly performed:

- purchasing management will not know which raw materials and components to purchase;
- public relations management will not know how to perform or improve its liaison function;
- financial management will not know how much funding is required; and
- human resource management will not know how many people to employ.

Summary

A business does not operate in isolation, and many factors contribute to a company's success. Marketing is a managerial process aimed at satisfying the needs and wants of customers, which are met by creating the correct products and services.

Marketing operates within a dynamic global environment, and is continually facing new challenges. The success of the marketing concept is now widely understood, spurring growth in non-profit marketing as these organisations begin using the tools and techniques of marketing management. The environment is changing as well, with almost every company being affected by rapid globalisation. The changing world economy, which has been sluggish for a long period of time, has resulted in more difficult times for both consumers and marketers. These challenges are intensified by demands that marketers conduct all of their business with stronger emphasis on ethics and social responsibility. Taken together, these changes define a new marketing landscape. Companies that succeed in this environment will have a strong focus on the changing marketplace and a total commitment to using the tools of marketing to provide real value to customers.[27]

References

1. Anon, 2008. *Entering a new market with a new product.* [Online] Available from: http://www.times100.co.uk/ (accessed: 14 July 2008).
2. Based on Lamb, CW, Hair, JF & McDaniel, C. 1998. *Marketing*, 4th ed. Ohio: South Western College Publishing, p 4.
3. Lamb et al, p 4.
4. Anon, 2008. *Entering a new market with a new product.* [Online] Available from: http://www.times100.co.uk/ (accessed: 14 July 2008).
5. American Marketing Association. 2005. *Marketing glossary dictionary.* [Online] Available from: http://www.marketingpower.com/mg-dictionary.php?SearchFor=marketing&Searched=1 (accessed: 14 February 2005).
6. Lamb et al, p 4.
7. Lamb et al, p 4.
8. Busch, PS & Houston, MJ. 1985. *Marketing: Strategic foundations.* Homewood, Ill: Richard, D Irwin Inc, p 15; Fin24. 2008. [Online] Available from: http://www.news24.com/News24/Technology/News/0,2-13-1443_2230329,00.html (accessed: 14 July 2008).
9. Cant, MC. 2004. *Essentials of marketing*, 2nd ed., pp 9–10.
10. Lamb et al, 2004. 7th ed., p 1; Kotler, P & Armstrong, G. 1996. *Principles of marketing*, 7th ed. Englewood Cliffs, NJ: Prentice Hall, p 16.
11. Lamb et al, 2004. 7th ed. p 2.
12. Lamb et al, 2004. 7th ed. p 2.
13. Van der Walt et al, p 20.
14. Du Plessis, PJ, Jooste, CJ & Strydom, JW. 2005. *Applied strategic marketing,* 2nd ed. Sandton: Heinemann, p 19.
15. Du Plessis et al, 2005, p 119.
16. Christopher, M, Payne, A & Ballantyne, D. 2003. *Relationship marketing: Creating stakeholder value.* Boston: Butterworth-Heinemann.
17. American Marketing Association. 2005. *Marketing glossary dictionary.* [Online] Available from: http://www.marketingpower.com/ (accessed: 15 February 2005).
18. Kotler, P & Armstrong, G. 2006. *Principles of marketing*, 11th ed. Englewood Cliffs, NJ: Prentice Hall, Inc, p 5.
19. Van der Walt et al; pp 27–30; American Marketing Association. 2005. *Marketing glossary dictionary.* [Online] Available from: http://www.marketingpower.com/ (accessed: 15 February 2005); Christopher, M, Payne, A & Ballantyne, D. 1991. *Relationship marketing*; Oxford: Heinemann, p 8; Cant, MC, op cit, p 18.
20. Cant, MC. 2004. *Essentials of marketing*, 2nd ed. p 19.
21. Van der Walt et al, pp 12–16.
22. American Marketing Association. 2005. *Marketing glossary dictionary.* [Online] Available from: http://www.marketingpower.com/ (accessed: 16 February 2005).

23. American Marketing Association. 2005. *Marketing glossary dictionary.* [Online] Available from: http://www.marketingpower.com/ (accessed: 16 February 2005).
24. American Marketing Association. 2005. *Marketing glossary dictionary.* [Online] Available from: http://www.marketingpower.com/ (accessed: 16 February 2005).
25. American Marketing Association. 2005. *Marketing glossary dictionary.* [Online] Available from: http://www.marketingpower.com/ (accessed: 16 February 2005).

CHAPTER TWO

The marketing environment

Learning outcomes

After you have studied this chapter you will be able to:

- explain the concept 'marketing environment';
- explain the interfaces between marketing management and the environment, namely the role of marketing management, and opportunities and threats in the environment;
- describe the composition of the marketing environment, namely the micro-, marketing and macro-environmental variables in the environment, and their implication for marketing management; and
- discuss alternative methods of environmental scanning.

2.1 Introduction

The previous chapter mentioned, inter alia, that marketing involves the extensive task of businesses seeking profits to survive and grow at all costs in a highly competitive market. Because the contemporary business has existed in an extremely unstable and turbulent environment in the past decade or two, a marketer can only survive, grow and make a profit if management understands what is going on in the environment. Instead of changing slowly and at a predictable pace, as in earlier decades such as the 1950s, the environment in which marketers find themselves at present holds many surprises and shocks.

Who would have thought that the average rand exchange rate against the US dollar would decline from R2,85 in 1993 to R4,29 in 1996, and at the time of writing was hovering at R8,00? How many marketers realised ten years ago, in planning their communication, that the black newspaper, *The Sowetan*, would have the highest circulation in the country? How many marketers would have thought that the turmoil in the economic markets would have such a dramatic influence on the South African economy in 2009?

Yet many marketers still do not realise the implications of this, especially when it comes to affirmative action, cultural and value shifts (which are more Afrocentric), and the questions surrounding the future economic order of South Africa. The surprises and shocks that the environment has in store for marketers are not confined to South Africa. Thus, for example, the American motor and electronics industries did not foresee Japan and other Asian countries' world domination of these industries. No one really understood the changes that the explosive growth of the Chinese and Indian markets would have on the world economy. This growth has, inter alia, resulted in a higher demand for basic materials and food, which has impacted negatively on developing economies such as South Africa who are, inter alia, paying more for oil and basic food commodities.

The so-called 'surprises' that the environment produces are nothing more than trends that appear and disappear, only to reappear in a different guise at a later stage. These trends or *external environmental variables* largely determine the success of the business's marketing efforts.

Thus the position of consumers and competitors in the market; relations with suppliers; economic, social and political trends; and numerous other events prevailing in the environment will, from time to time, threaten the successful existence of the business or, conversely, offer receptive and favourable conditions with good marketing opportunities.

Marketing management, however, does not deal exclusively with the external variables. Although marketing is also one of the main functions of the organisation and, in terms of the marketing concept, plays the principal role in its strategy formulation, the marketing activities should be performed in conjunction with other functional areas of the organisation and according to specific directives from top management. These directives refer more specifically to the mission, objectives and overall strategies formulated by top management to be pursued and supported by all the functional departments, including marketing management. Marketing management must also work closely with other departments to implement the marketing strategy. Those variables that concern marketing management within the business are known as the *internal environmental variables.*

The marketing environment is defined as *the sum total of the variables and forces inside as well as outside the business which influence marketing management's decisions.* This environment influences marketing management's ability to develop and execute successful strategies for its target market.

The successful management of marketing activities calls for an awareness on the part of marketing management of the internal and external variables of the environment which can affect the marketing efforts, and the marketing strategy, as indicated in figure 2.1, should be adapted on an ongoing basis to tie in with changes in the environment. Internal scanning is therefore necessary to determine the enterprise's strengths and weaknesses. External scanning is also necessary to gauge opportunities and threats (the SWOT approach). Of course, the aim here is to deploy the business's strengths and resources in the market in such a way that it can fully utilise opportunities and ward off any threats timeously.

In essence, environmental scanning is part of the formulation of the marketing strategy and part of the management strategy, and actually involves directing the business's resources towards satisfying the needs of the market which is the reason for the existence of the organisation.

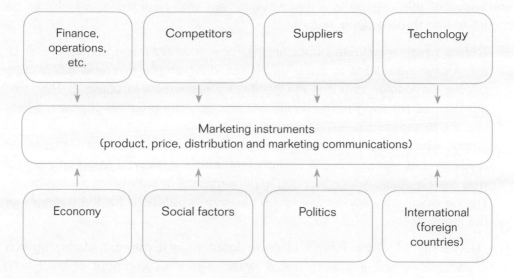

Figure 2.1 Environmental variables and marketing instruments

Timeous and continuous scanning (both inside and outside the business) of the total environment in which marketing management must operate is therefore a prerequisite for sound decision making about marketing strategy.

2.2 Marketing management and the marketing environment

2.2.1 Management and environmental change

The underlying problem for the successful survival of contemporary business in the global environment is the fact that the environment usually changes more quickly than the business is able to adapt. Hence the scanning of the marketing environment mainly revolves around change in the environment.

'Change' is a difficult term to define. Expressed simply, it is any alteration in the current situation of the organisation. This implies a change from a condition of stability to one of instability – a shift from the predictable to the unpredictable. It cannot be measured and causes uncertainty. No single factor can be held responsible for change and, in different places and communities, it occurs in different ways and at different rates.

Technological innovation, economic fluctuations, changing social values and demographic trends, political change. aggressive international competition and countless other variables are constantly changing the marketing environment, to such an extent that they not only affect the performance of businesses detrimentally but also threaten their existence. During the past decade, the structure of South African society and its lifestyles, values and expectations have changed perceptibly. Increasingly Afrocentric characteristics dominate the South African

environment. As a component of the environment, business expansion is therefore at the centre of environmental change and is constantly exposed to it. The
end result of this change is a new environment with new trends which can be
classified into three groups, namely:

- Trends which constitute opportunities for marketing management – that is,
  *a favourable situation in the environment in which the business has a com-
  petitive advantage and has the necessary resources to utilise it.* The main
  advantages resulting from change are probably the creation of new markets
  and the broadening of existing ones.
- Trends which pose particular threats to marketing management – that is, *an
  unfavourable situation in the environment which, if allowed to go unchecked,
  may have a detrimental effect on the performance or survival of the business.*
- Trends which may appear but which have *no implications* for the business or
  the industry.

The University of Cape Town's Unilever Institute of Strategic Marketing has
done research which indicates that a lucrative market segment of the South
African society has been ignored by South African businesses. This ignorance
just indicates the special kind of opportunities that still exist in the South African
market.

The 'Prime Time generation' – a lucrative market segment

There is a market segment in South Africa that needs to be targeted because
it has been forgotten by most businesses. This is the 40- to 50-year-old
urban consumer group that makes up 10% of the population but buys nearly
20% of all products and services. The combined income of this group is
estimated at nearly R300 billion, and is classified as LSM 7+. A significant
number of the members of this group are debt free (i.e. they are not paying
bonds). This group forms a lucrative segment to market to because they
have the time and money to enjoy life to the fullest.

Successful businesses that adapt to the environment are those that constantly
scan the environment and adjust their strategies to keep abreast of change and
to identify new opportunities, as described in the box above.

Adjusting strategies is therefore nothing more than those steps which marketing
management takes to gain a particular environmental fit for the organisation. Successful marketers do not delay their strategy adjustments until the environment
has changed so drastically that nothing can be done about it. They continually
scan the environment and management proactively.

A few comments on the role of marketing management in environmental scanning are necessary before the composition of the environment is examined.

2.2.2 Marketing management and the environment

Although the interaction between the organisation and its environment is the concern of the entire strategic management team, marketing management probably plays the most important role in this interaction. Support for this argument can be found, *firstly*, in the existence of a business mission statement, an important component which examines the business's product–market relationship. This entails a broad but clear indication of the business, product or service and at what market it is aimed. Both the business's product development and its market fall within the domain of marketing management, which necessitates its involvement in the development of the business's mission and strategy, as well as its involvement with the external environment.

A *second* reason for the importance of marketing management's involvement in the interaction between the business and its environment arises from the requirements that the marketing concept puts to management. It calls upon top management to determine the needs of the consumer and to satisfy them instead of deciding for the consumer what he or she needs.

Thirdly, marketing management plays a decisive role in the interface between the business and its environment because the latest trends in strategic management show that successful businesses are externally oriented – that is, they focus on the consumer, the competitor, the market and the market's environment.

One should also bear in mind that corporate planners depend on marketing management for ideas on new products and services and marketing opportunities, and that the marketing strategy (the consistency of the product, price, distribution and marketing communication elements as well as the extended elements of the service mix, namely people, processes and physical evidence) plays a decisive role in the total strategy.

The question that arises is how marketing management should become aware of and scan the infinite number of variables that can influence decision making. This is possible only if marketing management classifies and scans the numerous variables meaningfully. Before concentrating on scanning methods, it is necessary to conduct a meaningful classification of the variables in the marketing environment.

The composition of the environment in which marketing management operates, also called the marketing environment, will be discussed next.

2.3 The composition of the marketing environment

The introductory definition of the marketing environment stated that it is the sum total of the factors or variables and players which influence the ability of marketing management to successfully develop strategies for its target market. In order to scrutinise the multiplicity of environmental variables that influence marketing management, it is necessary to conduct a meaningful *classification* of the marketing environment to identify certain trends for further analysis in each group or *sub-environment*. Figure 2.2 shows the marketing model which indicates the composition of the marketing environment. It is clear from this figure that the total marketing environment comprises three principal components: the micro-, marketing and macro-environments. Each of these will now be examined.

2.4 The micro-environment

The first component of the total environment is the micro-environment or the internal environment, which comprises the organisation itself. Although this refers to those variables which are largely controlled by the organisation itself, such as its mission and objectives, its management structure, its resources and culture, one should remember that these variables are not solely under the control of marketing management.

As already mentioned, marketing management does have a significant influence on these variables, and marketing provides the central input in developing overall strategies, but it should be clear that while top management controls certain micro-variables, marketing management can also control some variables in the micro-environment.

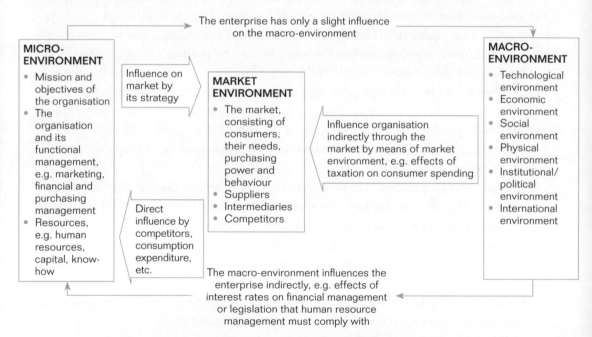

Figure 2.2 Composition of the marketing environment (the marketing environment model)
Source: Du Toit, GS, Erasmus, BJ & Strydom, JW (Eds). 2007. *Introduction to business management*. Cape Town: Oxford, p 93.

Although *top management* – that is, the executive management, which includes the functional managers – mainly focuses its decision making on the organisation's mission, objectives and overall strategies, there are four basic top management decisions which are of particular importance for marketing management: the *basic line of business* (product or service) of the organisation, the *overall goals* of the organisation, *the role of marketing management* in the above and *the role of the other management functions* in reaching the overall goals. Table 2.1 gives a brief description of the four basic decisions taken by top management.

Table 2.1 Variables in the micro-environment controlled by top management

Variable	Alternatives
1. Basic line of business (product or service)	
• Product/service category	Manufacturing, distributor, wholesaler
• Technology category	Tourism, fast food, clothing, hotel industry, computers
• Geographic category	Neighbourhood, city, region, province, national, international
• Ownership category	Sole proprietor, partnership, close corporation, public corporation
• Specific business category	e.g. City Lodge (hotel industry, national), Premier Foods (food, manufacture, national), Hatfield Bakery (bakery industry, Pretoria only)
2. Overall goals	
• Sales	Certain percentage increases per year or percentage market share
• Profit	Minimum percentage gross on net profit (on sales), profit ratios per product (patents), geographic area or rate of return on investment
• Customer acceptance	Environmentally friendly products and socially responsible products (toys and medicine)
3. The role of marketing management	
• Importance in the business	Line or staff functions, extensive budget and resources, role in strategy formulation
• Functions	Market research, planning, distribution, franchising
• Integration	Integration, decentralisation
4. The role of the other management functions	
• Human resources management	Determining responsibilites of each function, position of each in the organisational structure, relationship between functions, e.g. should operations management be responsible for purchasing or should purchasing do the procurement?
• Financial management	
• Operations management	
• Purchasing management	

The decisions controlled by top management ultimately reflect the mission and overall goals of the business organisation.

From these top management decisions, marketing management must determine the variables for which it is responsible. Table 2.2 briefly illustrates the micro-variables which fall under its control. In order to manage these variables effectively, marketing management must be well informed about the business's mission and top management's decisions regarding the overall goals and strategies.

Marketing management must therefore constantly scan the micro-environment. Marketing management's activities should also complement and support top management's decisions if the business is to function as a unit.

Table 2.2 Variables in the micro-environment controlled by marketing management

Variable	Alternatives
1. Selection of target market	
• Size	Mass market, specific market segment, geographic area
• Characteristics	Male, female, young, old, conservative, liberal
2. Marketing objectives	
• Sales	Brand loyalty, new products, new markets
• Profit	Profit ratio per product, area, quantity
• Image	Quality, friendly service
• Competitiveness	Competitive advantage through better product, lower price, extensive marketing communication
3. Organisational structure	
• Type	Functional, product, area
4. Marketing plan	
• Product/service	One basic model, one colour, sizes, styles
• Distribution	Direct, wholesale, cybermarketing/e-commerce
• Price	High, low, skimming
• Marketing communication	Advertising, personal selling, publicity
5. Control	Audit, cost analysis, control systems

In the introductory chapter, it was stated that marketing management's task mainly revolves around supplying an attractive product or service for target markets to provide a particular return for the business. It is clear from the above brief discussion of the micro-environment that marketing management's success is influenced mainly by what happens in the rest of the organisation, as well as occurrences in the market and macro-environments which affect the marketing effort. Hence marketing managers must not only study the needs of the target market but must also consider other variables and interest groups (functions) in the organisation, namely top management, financial management, operations management, purchasing management, and so on. All of these related interest groups constitute an organisation's internal or micro-environment.

Management decisions – including those made by marketing management and other management areas – influence the market environment by extending or indeed curtailing the strategies employed to maintain the business's market share.

2.5 The market environment

The second sub-component of the marketing environment is the market environment, which is found just outside the organisation. In this environment, all the variables depicted in figure 2.2 are relevant to virtually every organisation because they determine the nature and strength of the competition in any industry. The key variables in this environment are the following:

- *Consumers* with a particular buying power and behaviour, which in turn determine the number of entrants to the market.
- *Competitors* who are established in the market and wish to maintain or improve their position, including existing, new and potential competitors.
- *Intermediaries* who compete against each other to handle the business's products, or wish to handle only those of competitors.
- *Suppliers* who provide or do not wish to provide products, raw materials, services and even financing to the business.

All these variables create particular *opportunities* and *threats.* Although marketing management can influence certain variables by adjusting its strategy, it has no control over these variables.

The market environment has a strong influence on the success or failure of the business. A case in point is a strong competitor who possesses the necessary ability to enter into a price war or launch a new substitute product. The principal task of marketing management in this environment is therefore to identify, evaluate and utilise opportunities that arise in the market and then to develop its strategies in order to meet competition. For these reasons, the market environment is also called the *task environment.* The market environment is also influenced by developments in the macro-environment, ultimately to reach the market environment.

2.5.1 Consumers

The market consists of people with specific needs that have to be satisfied and who have the financial ability to satisfy them.

This explains why consumers with their particular needs, buying power and behaviour are the chief component of the market environment. The market, or the consumers in the market environment, are in fact the ultimate target at which marketing management aims the business's market offering. In a study and analysis of the market (primarily by means of market research as discussed in chapter 3), marketing management should bear in mind that there are five groups of consumers or markets.

2.5.1.1 Consumer markets

In these markets, individuals and households purchase products and services for personal consumption. In studying the consumer market, marketing management therefore firstly analyses the number of consumers in a particular area. The total

South African consumer market, for example, is represented by the number of inhabitants. The population in South Africa is expected to increase to 51,5 million by 2021 (see table 2.3). Furthermore, the population spread of South Africans per province is depicted in table 2.4.

Table 2.3 Population projection in South Africa, 2005–2021

Year	African	Asian	Coloured	White	Total
2005	36 880 005	1 152 384	3 999 901	5 208 408	47 240 698
2006	37 109 455	1 161 612	4 036 380	5 198 269	47 505 716
2007	37 300 881	1 170 184	4 068 544	5 184 539	47 724 148
2008	37 481 349	1 178 069	4 096 315	5 167 606	47 923 339
2009	37 654 959	1 185 317	4 119 802	5 147 583	48 107 661
2010	37 839 207	1 191 826	4 139 083	5 124 805	48 294 921
2011	38 036 155	1 197 587	4 154 597	5 099 416	48 487 755
2012	38 248 188	1 202 638	4 167 651	5 072 127	48 690 604
2013	38 486 905	1 206 959	4 177 979	4 177 979	48 914 812
2014	38 750 152	1 210 586	4 186 561	5 012 324	49 159 622
2015	39 043 456	1 213 550	4 194 231	4 980 891	49 432 128
2016	39 356 893	1 215 912	4 201 715	4 949 104	49 723 624
2017	39 693 290	1 217 746	4 209 758	4 917 163	50 037 957
2018	40 057 637	1 219 090	4 218 713	4 885 383	50 380 822
2019	40 445 466	1 219 986	4 228 614	4 853 600	50 747 665
2020	40 857 487	1 220 452	4 239 152	4 821 400	51 138 490
2021	41 230 385	1 220 517	4 250 025	4 788 935	51 549 834

Table 2.4 shows the distribution of the population across the nine provinces.

Table 2.4 Population estimates of South Africa across the nine provinces, 2008

Province	Number (in millions)
Eastern Cape	6,58
Free State	2,88
Gauteng	10,45
KwaZulu-Natal	10,11
Limpopo	5,27
Mpumalanga	3,59
Northern Cape	1,13
North West	3,43
Western Cape	5,26
Total	**48,69**

Source: Statistics South Africa. *Mid-year population estimates.* Statistical release, P0302, 31 July 2008, p 5.

Besides the number of consumers in a particular area or market segment analysed to estimate the market, a significant component of the consumer market is the *buy-*

ing power of the consumers. Buying power is represented mainly by the *personal disposable income* of consumers. Personal disposable income is that portion of personal income that remains after deducting direct tax, plus credit (loans from banks, shops and other institutions), which can therefore be used to purchase consumer products and services. Table 2.5 indicates the per capita income in this regard of the South African population according to the major race groups.

Table 2.5 The per capita income of South African consumers according to the four race groups

Monthly household earnings (rands)	Average per capita income within household income band (rands)				
	African	Coloured	Indian	White	Total
R0 – 800	75,11	54,83	24,30	8,32	69,51
R801 – 1,200	522,39	406,85	309,01	650,36	513,17
R1 201 – 2,500	908,57	637,63	770,99	991,33	851,08
R2 501 – 6,000	1 650,80	1 206,86	1 620,47	1 812,70	1 574,65
R6 001 – 16,000	3 252,97	2 899,05	3 105,70	4 518,46	3 634,08
R16 000 plus	8 567,27	6 734,86	8 700,42	10 832,24	9 737,55

Source: Statistics South Africa. 2006 *General household survey 2005*. Pretoria, Cape Town: Statistics South Africa. Analysis by Debbie Budlender, Centre for Actuarial Research, UCT. Source: As presented in Leatt, A. *Income poverty in South Africa*, p 28.

Only two of the main characteristics of the consumer market – the number of consumers and the buying power of consumers – are mentioned above. Numerous other characteristics such as language, age structure, gender distribution, marital status, family size and literacy influence the spending patterns of the consumer market.

The consumer market can also be grouped into *durable products* (e.g. furniture, household appliances, cars), *semi-durable products* (e.g. clothing, shoes, car tyres), *non-durable products* (e.g. food, tobacco) and *services* (e.g. insurance, rent, communication).

This classification enables marketing management to analyse specific segments of the market.

2.5.1.2   Industrial markets

Industrial markets (also called B2B markets) are markets in which manufacturing organisations buy products and services for their own consumption and/or use in the production of further products or services. This expenditure by the industrial market therefore involves capital goods (machinery, plant and heavy equipment), investment and inventory, and the consumption of raw materials.

2.5.1.3   Government markets

In South Africa, government markets refer to purchases by the general government, and the provinces and local authorities. The marketing of products and services in industrial and government markets differs from that in the consumer market.

2.5.1.4 Resale markets

Resale markets refer to businesses that purchase products and services in order to resell them at a profit. This entails trade in a particular country or area, referring, among other things, to the wholesale, the retail and the liquor trade.

2.5.1.5 International markets

International markets refer to foreign buyers, which include consumers, manufacturers, resellers and government. Table 2.6 reflects statistics regarding South Africa's exports and imports. Note the positive trade balance for this period.

The preceding discussion of the different markets shows why the market environment is such an important component of the environment for marketing management. Without a continuous study and analysis of this component, marketing management cannot succeed.

Table 2.6 International trade dimensions of South Africa

Indicator	1997	1998	1999	2000	2001	2002	2003	2004	2005	2006	2007
Exports	131,5	144,9	165,5	210,4	251,3	314,1	275,6	296,2	331,4	396,5	494,4
Imports	127,9	144,2	147,4	187,6	216,0	275,4	258,8	306,9	351,7	465,0	563,4
Trade balance	3 596,3	782 042	18 199,4	22 765,3	35 297,3	38 674,2	16 742,4	-10 680,8	-20 259,7	-68 511,4	-69 090,8

Source: South Africa Reserve Bank. 2008. *South African trade chapter.* [Online] Available from: http://www.dti.gov.za/econdb/raportt/raptottr.html (accessed: 2 September 2008).

In addition to consumers, who form markets, marketing management should keep abreast of the other components of the market environment.

2.5.2 Competitors

The contemporary business organisation operates within a market economy and is characterised by competition in the market environment. This means that every organisation trying to sell a product or service in the market environment is constantly faced with competitors who often determine how much of a given product can be marketed and at what price. Moreover, organisations not only compete for a share in the market for their product, but also with other organisations for labour, capital, entrepreneurship and material.

As a variable in the market environment, *competition* can be defined as *a situation in the market environment in which several organisations with more or less the same products or services compete for the support of the same consumers.* The result of this competition is that the market mechanism keeps excessive profits in check, acts as an incentive to higher productivity and encourages technological innovation. However, although the consumers benefit from competition, it is nevertheless a variable that management has to take into account in its entry into the operations in the market.

In its assessment of competition, marketing management must bear in mind that the nature and intensity of competition in a particular market environment are determined by five factors:

1. The possibility of new entrants or departures (competitors).
2. The bargaining power of clients and consumers.
3. The bargaining power of suppliers.
4. The availability or even lack of substitute products or services.
5. The number of existing competitors.

Figure 2.3 illustrates the five-forces model responsible for competition in a particular industry. The collective strength of these five forces determines the competitiveness in the industry and therefore the profitability of the industry. Competition varies from intense in industries such as tyres and retailing, to moderate in mining and cold-drinks. The weaker the five forces, the better the chances are of success. In spite of the collective strength of the five forces, marketing management still has the task of finding a position in the industry where the business can best defend itself against these forces.

The alternative would be for marketing management to create a position in which the business could influence these forces in its favour. Market segmentation and positioning are discussed in greater detail in chapter 5. Continuous scanning of the competition provides the basis for the development of the marketing strategy. It emphasises the critical strengths and weaknesses of the business, gives an indication of the positioning decisions which must be taken, singles out the areas where strategic changes can contribute the highest returns, and focuses on industry trends in terms of opportunities and threats.

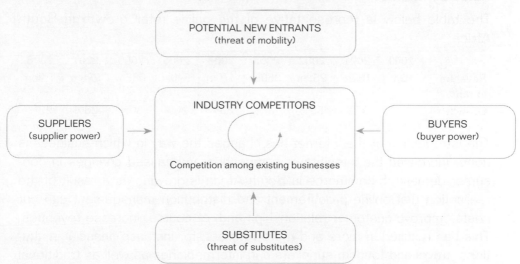

Figure 2.3 Competitive forces in an industry (Porter's five-forces model)

Source: Porter, ME. 1985. *Competitive advantage: Creating and sustaining superior performance.* Quoted in Kotler, P. 1997. *Marketing management: Analysis, planning, implementation and control.* Englewood Cliffs, NJ: Prentice Hall, p 229.

2.5.3 Intermediaries

Besides consumers and competitors in the market environment, intermediaries also play a vital role in bridging the gap or distance between the manufacturer and the consumer.

By bridging this gap, place, time and ownership utility are created. Intermediaries are wholesalers and retailers, commercial agents and brokers and, in the Third World, even spaza stores. Among all these intermediaries there are also financial intermediaries such as banks and insurers who, from a financial angle, are also involved in the transfer of products and services.

Decision making by marketing management regarding intermediaries is complicated by the following:

- *The dynamic and ever-changing nature of intermediaries.* New trends in turnover or consumption are responsible for the development of new types of intermediaries. Examples of contemporary South African trends in this regard are extended shopping hours, the power shift from the manufacturer to large retailer because of barcoding and house brands, increasing advertising by shopping centres themselves, the growing importance of large shopping centres in black residential areas, and the pressure on the smaller shops such as the spaza stores and informal retailers such as hawkers. The growth of e-commerce in South Africa poses drastic changes to the structure of competition between intermediaries, as depicted in the box below.

Sales by Internet[7]

The table below is representative of the online retail growth in South Africa

	2000	2001	2002	2003	2004	2005	2006	2007	2008
Revenue in rand	82m	162m	252m	350m	470m	540m	688m	928m	1,2bn
Growth		97%	55%	40%	33%	20%	30%	35%	29%

The introduction of the Internet has changed the way in which business is done, increased the intensity of competition and caused changes in consumer demand. E-commerce in South Africa is growing as a result of the realisation that online procurement and distribution management can cut costs, improve customer relationships and, of course, increase revenues. This has resulted in more and more retailers, for instance financial institutions, travel and tourism suppliers and intermediaries as well as traditional retailers (e.g. Pick n Pay), distributing their product offerings online. The online sale of airline tickets is the leading e-commerce business.

➲

➲
The example of kulula.com

Since kulula.com's impressive entrance into the domestic airline market and its bold online presence, competition in the industry has become rather exciting.

In South Africa, kulula.com was one of the first retailers to brave the quest of distributing its product online, and since 2001 the airline has come a long way. By 2004, kulula.com had captured 20% of the local market share and earned the reputation of being South Africa's biggest online retailer. One of the main reasons attributed to this success is the ease of booking on the airline's website. Not only can one make a reservation for an air ticket online, but kulula.com's comprehensive online booking system now gives consumers the option to book other travel amenities too, allowing them to buy complete travel packages online.

To date, kulula.com has managed to maintain its position as South Africa's biggest online retailer. Each day the kulula.com website services seven million visitors, generating over R1,3 billion in revenue annually for the airline.

• *Decisions about intermediaries mean the formation of long-term alliances.* This may have certain implications for the marketing strategy. Thus the power of large retailers may have specific implications for price and advertising decisions, and product diversification is dependent on the capacity of intermediaries. The new trends among intermediaries offer challenges for marketing management, but certain trends can also imply threats.

2.5.4 Suppliers

An enterprise is not concerned only with marketing its product but also requires inputs from the market environment. These inputs are primarily material, including raw materials, equipment, energy, capital and labour, which are provided by suppliers. From a marketing perspective, the purchase of products for resale is a critical input on the part of suppliers. When it is realised that about 60 cents (60%) in every rand paid out by the business is spent on purchases from suppliers, the importance thereof as a variable in the market environment becomes clear. If a business cannot obtain the necessary inputs of the required quality in the right quantity and at the right price for the achievement of its objectives, it cannot hope to achieve success in a competitive market environment.

In the case of *materials*, practically every business, whether it is in manufacturing, trading or contracting, depends on regular supplies. As in the case of raw materials, there are suppliers of *capital*, an input upon which the business is dependent for its survival. Banks, building societies and shareholders are such suppliers. Small organisations, in particular, often find it extremely difficult to attract the necessary capital.

2.5.5 Opportunities and threats in the market environment

The changes brought about in the market environment by variables and their interactions, and the trends that constantly develop in the macro-environment, can ultimately be classified into two groups: those that offer an *opportunity* and those that pose a *threat*.

An *opportunity* may be defined as a *favourable condition or tendency in the market environment which can be utilised to the benefit of the organisation by means of a deliberate management effort*. It should, however, be clearly understood that the possibilities inherent in an opportunity always have to be assessed against the background of the organisation's resources and capabilities. Without the necessary capacities and resources, an opportunity cannot be properly utilised. The success of a business in making good use of an opportunity therefore depends upon its ability to satisfy the requirement for success in that particular market.

In contrast to the environmental opportunity, an environmental *threat* may be defined as an *unfavourable condition or tendency in the market environment that can, in the absence of a deliberate effort by management, lead to the failure of the business, its product or its service*.

In view of the constant changes in the market environment, it is the duty of management to identify such threats, both actual and potential, and to develop a counter-strategy or contingency strategy to meet them.

The market environment entails an interaction between an organisation and its suppliers, consumers and competitors with alternative marketing offerings. The interaction can result in opportunities or threats to a business, and marketing management must be aware of trends in the market environment so that management can utilise opportunities profitably and avoid threats in good time. For this purpose, environmental scanning, marketing research and information management are the proper instruments.

2.6 The macro-environment

2.6.1 The composition of the macro-environment

Apart from the market environment, which has a direct effect on the fortunes of a business, a wider macro-environment exists, containing variables that directly or indirectly exert an influence on the business and its market environment. These variables constitute those uncontrollable forces in the environment that are sometimes referred to as *megatrends*. As can be seen from figure 2.2, the literature on management divides the macro-environment into six variables, namely technological, economic, social, physical, institutional/political and international (or sub-environments). The technological environment is responsible for the rate of innovation and change. The economic environment involves factors such as inflation, recessions and exchange rates, and the monetary and fiscal policies that influence the welfare of the business and its community. The social environment concerns the individual's way of life, customs and standards formed by his or her culture, and these also make certain demands on the business. The physical environment comprises natural resources as well as the improvements made by people, for example roads and bridges, mineral wealth, and flora and fauna. The institutional environment embraces the government with its political involvement and legislation as the main components, and, finally, the international environment concerns local and foreign political trends and events that influence organisations and the market environment.

2.6.2 The technological environment

History as we know it dates back approximately 5 000 years, and drastic changes occurred along the way. The products which exist today, excluding a few basic products, were developed during the past 60 years. And the latest products which have already become indispensable to modern society, such as laser surgery, robotics, silicon protein molecules and fibre optics, and about 80% of today's medicines are the products of the last ten years! This tremendous environmental change is largely a manifestation of technological innovation, a process which enlarges the capabilities of mankind.

Technological innovation originates in research and development by business as well as the state, and results not only in new machinery or products but also in new processes and methods, and even new approaches to management that bring about change in the environment. Even the social and institutional progress in a country and the structures it possesses relate to technology. Technological innovation also affects other environmental variables. The economic growth rate is influenced by the number of new inventions as well as social change, for example the appearance of a new product such as television brings about a revolution in people's way of life. These variables in turn influence technology, and so the process of innovation and change is repeated.

Every new technological development or innovation creates opportunities and threats in the environment. Television was a threat to films and newspapers, but at the same time presented opportunities for instant meals (i.e. TV dinners), satellite communication and the advertising industry. The opportunities created by computers in banking, manufacturing, transport and practically every industry are innumerable. In the box that follows is an illustration of the use of the Internet as a technology revolution.

Moreover, technological or scientific innovation often has unpredictable consequences: the contraceptive pill meant smaller families and more women at work, and therefore more disposable income for families to spend on holidays and luxury articles which may previously not have been possible. The most outstanding characteristic of technological innovation is probably the fact that it constantly accelerates the rate of change.

Marketing management has a threefold involvement in the process of techno-logical innovation and change. *Firstly*, it promotes technological innovation when it identifies new consumer needs and when it influences technology in such a way that it leads to the satisfaction of those needs. *Secondly,* it distributes technologi-cal innovation throughout society – that is, marketing tracks down new inventions and then develops and commercialises them. *Thirdly,* marketing management is involved in scanning technological progress and the opportunities and threats that it poses for the business.

Technological trends that organisations must consider

Some of the unique characteristics of the technological environment in which organisations operate are as follows:

- *Accelerating the pace of technological change.* Many of the products that we use today have only been around for the past decade or so. The rate of change is accelerating, which brings unique opportunities and threats for organisations. The use of the Internet, cellphones and other media has made it possible to work from home – a trend that has special opportunities to reduce pollution through travel and opens up new opportunities for tele-shopping.
- *Unlimited opportunities for innovation.* New generation technologies such as robotics and biotechnology create opportunities for longevity and improved food.
- *No increase in expenditure on research and development (R&D).* Even the US, which was at the forefront of R&D, is proceeding with more caution. More and more companies are happy to be followers, making minor modifications to existing products.
- *Increasing regulation regarding technological change.* With the growing complexity of products, more and more government regulation is aimed to safeguard customers against potentially unsafe products.

Marketing management therefore has a significant task to perform in managing the transition to a new technology because technological innovation can have a fast and drastic effect on a product or industry. A case in point is the detrimen-tal influence of quartz watches on the manufacturing of conventional watches. However, this does not mean that a certain technological innovation will render the older technology obsolete. Various observations have been made in this regard:

- A new technological advancement does not necessarily smother an old technology, but can even stimulate its growth because the threatened organisations improve their old technologies. Safety razor sales, for example, have actually increased 800% since the advent of the electric razor.
- In most cases, firms involved in the old technology have a substantial amount of time to react to the new technology.
- It is relatively difficult to predict the outcome of a new technology, and it tends to create new markets instead of encroaching on existing ones. For example, disposable ballpoint pens created a new market without killing it for refillable ones.
- A further characteristic that marketing management should bear in mind is that technological innovations are unlimited and that they continuously affect the environment.

In scanning the technological environment, marketing management must keep in mind the maturity of an existing technology, and its possible replacement with a new one. Technological innovation is especially possible when:

- the physical boundaries of an existing technology are reached;
- research and development in a certain area become uneconomical; and
- competitors start to experiment with expensive and risky technology.

Technological progress, therefore, affects the business as a whole, including its product, life cycle, supply of materials, production processes and management approach, and ultimately its position in the market. Hence marketing management should be increasingly alert to technological changes.

2.6.3   The economic environment

After technology, which is primarily responsible for change in the environment, comes the economy, which is influenced by technology, politics, and the social and international environments, while it in turn also asserts some influence on these variables. These cross-influences cause ongoing change in the economic growth rate, levels of employment, consumer income, the inflation rate and the general state of the economy, which is indicated by either prosperity or adversity. Ultimately, these economic forces will have implications for the business and marketing management. The main interfaces between the economic environment and the business are the economic growth rate, consumer income, inflation, monetary and fiscal policy, and fluctuations in these magnitudes.

The economic well-being of a community is measured by the range and number of products and services produced. Expressed in financial terms, this standard is equivalent to the gross domestic product (GDP) – that is, *the total value of finished products and services produced within the borders of a country during a given period, usually a year.*

During the 30 years after World War II, the average real growth of the South African GDP was about 4,7% per annum, after which, from 1970 to 1988, it declined to an average annual rate of 2,8%, and thereafter to even lower levels. The GDP for 1996 was 3,1%, dropping to 1,7% for 1997, while the GPD for 2008 was estimated at 4%.

For the past number of years the South Africa's population growth of 2,5% was lower than the growth in the GDP, which means that the standard of living of South Africans has generally improved. The unknown factor, however, is the influx of immigrants from neighbouring states and rising unemployment figures as at the time of writing (2009) South Africa faces its first long-term economic decline phase.

The unemployment rates per province are depicted in table 2.7.

Table 2.7 Unemployment rates per province (2001 to 2004)

Unemployment rate	Percent (%)			
	2001	2002	2003	2004
Western Cape	20,9	20,9	22,0	19,2
Eastern Cape	30,6	28,1	33,3	35,8
Northern Cape	23,8	24,3	25,0	19,7
Free State	27,4	27,7	27,5	22,6
KwaZulu-Natal	26,2	28,1	28,2	25,9
North West	27,9	24,3	26,8	24,9
Gauteng	28,2	29,8	31,2	28,3
Mpumalanga	26,3	22,2	23,3	19,1
Limpopo	28,1	38,2	42,3	33,3
South Africa	**26,4**	**27,7**	**29,3**	**26,4**

Source: Statistics South Africa. 2008. *Labour force survey historical revision: March series, 2001 to 2007, report 0210.* [Online] Available from: http://www.statssa.gov.za/qlfs/docs/March_Series_Historical_revisions.pdf (accessed: 2 September 2008), p 6.

Although the economic growth rate has a decisive effect on marketing management, it is the correct gauging of the upswing and downswing phases of the economy that has a significant influence on marketing strategy. If an organisation is expecting a recession, it can benefit by reducing inventory timeously because its stocks could be difficult to sell, by maintaining a state of liquidity to avoid the high cost of interest or by postponing any ideas of expansion indefinitely. In the case of an upswing, a sound strategy would be to build up sufficient inventory in good time and carry out whatever expansion is necessary to meet increased demand.

Inflation, like growth, is an economic variable that influences the decisions made by management. An inflation rate of more than 10% has been a regular phenomenon since the 1970s. The average inflation rate has declined since 1993, with an inflation rate of below 10% from 1993 onwards. In 2007 and 2008 we saw a return of strong inflation increases with the inflation rate calculated for May 2008 at 10,9%. South Africa's inflation rate is, however, still higher than her main trading partners. Hence it is the task of management to constantly study the effect of inflation on products and services, or rather the implications thereof on the marketing strategy.

The effects of inflation on the business are profound. For example, it causes bogus profit, while making inroads into capital. It makes cost accounting and the financing of credit difficult. It forces the industrial buyer to build up supplies, while consumers adjust their behaviour to take account of keener price competition, increasing the importance of functionalism and buying early in anticipation of price rises – which often leads to another round of inflationary demand. Inflationary pressures in South Africa are expected to remain reasonably high for the next ten years, the most pressure coming from the wage demands of trade unions. In the long term this will result in new consumer values, spending and impoverishment. However, new values also mean new opportunities and new markets.

How businesses deal with periods of high inflation

Regarding the holding of inventory, the old way of thinking was to minimise costs. In a period of steep increases in manufacturing costs it may now be better to keep more stock as a hedge to further price increases. Additional to this, sourcing from farther-away suppliers will be more unattractive with transportation costs the main reason upon which decisions will be based.

With the aggregate demand for products and services in deadlines organisations must be careful in using the cost-plus approach to increase prices. If the customer is prepared to pay the additional amount then the organisation is happy. Unfortunately more-and-more customers are not prepared to pay more due to salary increases below the inflation rate and job losses. Organisations therefore have to be careful to adapt prices over time with small but regular increases below the inflation rate.

Organisations further promote products where no price increases have been done whilst not advertising those products which have seen prices increased a lot. Grocery retailers promote their private-label or 'no-name' products. Counter to normal practices, organisations should advertise more in inflationary times when most competitors are cutting back on advertising, as this will mean more exposure.

Another economic variable affecting a business and its market environment is the government's monetary policy, in accordance with which the money supply, interest rates and the position of a country's monetary unit are relative to the disturbances that other countries' monetary units can cause in the environment. Fiscal policy affects both the business and the consumer through taxation rates and tax reforms.

These economic trends which were briefly discussed as a few examples of economic change demand a constant awareness by marketing management, and regular consideration of the mission and strategy of the organisation.

2.6.4 *The social environment*

The environmental variable probably most subject to the influence of other variables, especially technology and the economy, is social change. Precisely because it affects management indirectly through people as consumers and employees, the ultimate effect of social change on the strategy of an organisation should not be underestimated.

People are the products of their community: as members of a particular community they accept and assimilate its language, its values, its faith, its expectations, its laws and its customs. This culture, the sum total of the way of life of a group of people, influences the individual's way of life. Thus consumption cannot be explained solely in economic terms – the effects of culture and social change must also be considered. However, culture is not static, but over time changes a community's values, expectations, lifestyle and customs.

The culture of a particular country is also not completely homogeneous. There are also many subcultures based on such things as nationality, religion, population group or geographic area, each of which entails a distinctive change in the environment with further implications for management.

Changes in the use of the English language

In Shakespeare's time only 150 000 of the 450 000 words now part of the English language existed. Were he alive today, he would understand only five words out of nine.

The business stands at the centre of social change. On the one hand, it contributes to social change, while on the other, it should constantly be aware of the major influences of social currents on itself. We shall now briefly examine a few observable social trends. Demographic change – that is, change in the growth and the composition of populations – is probably the social variable that causes the most change in the market by altering people's way of life.

In this regard, Western societies are characterised by failing population growth rates and shrinking families, with the emphasis on smaller consumer units.

There are growing numbers of one-person households, and consequently there is a rising demand for services. There is an increasing population of ageing and more affluent people, and families with members over the age of 65, who create special marketing opportunities. Single-parent families are also on the rise, with definite implications for the market and for the social responsibilities of the business.

In contrast to the above, developing communities are characterised by high population growth rates, of which the largest percentage is under the age of 18, declining standards of living with a waning demand for basic consumer goods, and no demand for services. Table 2.8 represents the growth rate of the South African population to the year 2006 while table 2.9 depicts the 2006 population groups per gender and race group.

Table 2.8 Annual population growth rates of the South African population 2001–2006 per gender

	2001–2002	2002–2003	2003–2004	2004–2005	2005–2006
Male	1,27	1,24	1,21	1,20	1,09
Female	1,23	1,20	1,16	1,14	1,02
Total	1,25	1,22	1,19	1,17	1,06

Table 2.8 shows that the implied rate of growth for the South African population has been declining steadily between 2001 and 2006. The overall growth rate for 2005–2006 is estimated at 1,06%, with the rate for females slightly lower than that of males.

Table 2.9 Population groups per gender and race (2006)

Population group	Male		Female		Total	
	Number	% of total pop	Number	% of total pop	Number	% of total pop
African	18 558 500	79,6	19 104 400	79,4	37 662 900	79,5
Coloured	2 060 000	8,8	2 138 800	8,9	4 198 800	8,9
Indian/Asian	570 200	2,4	593 700	2,5	1 163 900	2,5
White	2 138 900	9,2	2 226 400	9,3	4 365 300	9,2
Total	23 327 600	100	24 063 300	100	47 390 900	100

Source: Statistics South Africa. 2006. *Mid-year population estimates, South Africa 2006.* Statistical release P0302, p 6.

Demographic trends that influence the purchase of products and services are the following:

* *Urbanisation,* employment and the ability to provide housing, food and urban services. Less-developed countries are characterised by phenomenal growth in urbanisation, growing unemployment, increasing pollution and the growth of informal settlements, where it is a question of merely satisfying basic needs.
* *The changing population composition* in developed countries provides a significant over-65 market for housing, insurance, health care and tourism. In less-developed countries, there is an increasing juvenile segment of the market with less spending power.
* *The increasing economic power of women* with wider interests outside the home, more disposable income and less time to buy.

- *The increase in the number of households* because of the rise in the divorce rate. Smaller and more households mean a larger market for household equipment, products and services.

Another social variable with clear implications for management is the changing role of women in society. As recently as 15 years ago, 60% of American women believed that a woman's place was in the home. Nowadays, only 22% are of that opinion.

Working women are regarded as the decisive factor in the development of supermarkets, extended shopping hours and takeaway meals. With a greater disposable income and less time to buy, they are prepared to pay for convenience.

These developments entail changes in the lives of women and consequently of their families, and also affect their buying patterns by shifting women's shopping hours mostly to weekends, and causing women to favour shopping centres catering for practically all their needs under one roof. This trend also puts new pressure on management for equal opportunities for women in management and to provide day-care facilities for the children of working mothers. The demand for 'convenience products' affects management particularly.

A further trend that has to be considered is *consumerism,* the social force that protects the consumer by exerting legal, moral, economic and even political pressure on management. This movement is a natural consequence of a better-educated public that resists such things as misleading advertisements, unsafe products, and profiteering and other objectionable practices, and presses for the rights of the consumer. These aspects are discussed in chapter 4.

The final aspect of the social environment that merits attention is the pressure society exerts on the organisation, forcing it to be socially responsible. This means that organisations should act responsibly in the environment in which they operate and constantly consider the consequences of their decisions and actions. In many respects, criticism of the actions of organisations such as misleading advertising, dangerous products, pollution of the environment and exploitation of the consumer are levelled at marketing management, probably because marketing is responsible for providing the ultimate product or service.

'Black diamonds' lose shine

The rise in interest rates, inflation and food and fuel prices has hit all sectors of South African society. Consumers and retailers are feeling pain; this is evident, for example, in the growing number of repossessions and the recent downturn in the car market. However, a research survey by the TNS Research group shows that the biggest sufferers to date have been the members of the emerging black middle class, South Africa's so-called 'black diamonds'.

➲

↻

Between August 2007 and August 2008, 10% of the black middle class had items repossessed. Results from the TNS survey showed that 20% of those surveyed never seemed to be able to pay off their debts, while 50% had outstanding bills on retail accounts leading to the growing number of repossessions in South African. Consequently, black diamonds are starting to feel the pressure of the credit meltdown.

With an interest rate of 12%, consumers are struggling to meet repayments on car loans. Evidence of this is the 6 000 repossessed vehicles (ranging from Aston Martins to sports utility vehicles) that are being handed over by banks to Aucor Auctioneers each month. The new-car market is also feeling the brunt as sales of new vehicles have dropped to their lowest level in four years.

It is not only car owners and the automobile industry; homeowners are also struggling to meet bond payments, leading to 2 000 homes being repossessed every month.

Ms T Motaung (36), classified as a black diamond, is a manager of a legal firm in South Africa and lives in Gauteng. She is an example of a consumer who fell behind in meeting her high loan repayments on both her house and car. Repossession was the reality and she was forced to give up her Audi A4.

2.6.5 The physical environment

The physical environment embraces the limited resources from which the business obtains its raw materials, as well as the environment into which it discharges its waste, This has a bearing on various forms of pollution. Since the 1960s, there has been growing concern about our natural environment, particularly with regard to a shortage of resources, protest against all forms of pollution and the destruction of the environment by opencast mining and the building of roads and dams, and speculation about whether the theories of Malthus and others regarding the overpopulation of the earth are in fact being confirmed. Business itself has developed an awareness of the physical environment, because this can affect the organisation in many ways. Certain interfaces that present opportunities as well as threats to the business can be discerned.

- The *first* interface involves a broad range of resources that are becoming increasingly scarce, such as raw materials, energy and foodstuffs. These have certain implications for management. Shortages affect the supply of goods, contribute to inflation and cause severe price rises, and often necessitate different methods of manufacturing and a reorientation of marketing thought in an effort to find substitutes for unobtainable products.

By the year 2030, 60% of the world's population will be living in cities, a 10% increase since 2007. According to a United Nations report, growth in developing countries like China, India and others in Africa is rapidly increasing, with the equivalent of a city the size of Vancouver being built every week – putting ecologically rich areas at risk.

Source: Science Daily. 2008. *Global impact of urbanization Threatening world's biodiversity and natural resources.* [Online] Available from: http://www.sciencedaily.com/releases/2008/06/080610182856.htm

- The *second* interface is the increasing cost of energy, which also influences the environment with consequent opportunities and threats for the business. The rise in the price of oil, from $2 a barrel in 1970 to $34 in 1982, to over $150 a barrel in 2008, set in motion a frantic search for alternative sources of energy. Coal was once again in great demand, to the extent that South Africa became second only to Poland as a coal exporter. Research on solar, wind and nuclear power was intensified, and the costs of nuclear power were studied. South Africa is fairly rich in energy sources with 10% of the world's coal reserves, 18% of the Western world's uranium reserves, the Sasol plants and some gas and oil off the southern Cape coast.

South Africa's electricity crisis

South Africa has endured an electricity crisis which caused blackouts and so-called 'load shedding'. This is as a result of many factors, but mainly caused by poor planning. Of the many reasons for this crisis, only those relating to the physical environment will be briefly discussed.

According to many, the tight electricity supply to consumers had everything to do with Eskom's negligence in securing enough usable coal for its power stations. The power crisis that the country is currently experiencing may have been as a result of bad decisions made by Eskom management regarding its coal stock years ago. It emerged that inadequate coal supplies and low, stretched-out stockpiles played a significant role in reducing generation supply. In 2001 the decision was made to reduce coal stockpile levels in order to reduce working capital and related holding costs. To illustrate this point, Eskom had 19,8 million tons of coal in stock for 61 days of burn in 2000, and despite the rise in electricity demand, in just a year the stockpile had been reduced by five million tons to 14,8 million tons, only 44 days of burn by the end of 2001. At one time in 2008, the stockpile dropped even further to an average of only 12 days of coal to burn.

➲

↪

Although coal is a critical source of electricity generation, it is believed that the reason for the blackouts is that Eskom did not extend the long-term contracts of its coal suppliers. Rather, Eskom procured cheap coal supplies sourced from small, inexperienced as well as expensive suppliers for the sake of black economic empowerment (BEE). Eskom was keen to move away from long-term contracts with its original suppliers and rather to create an 'active coal spot market'. In 2002 it was approved that Eskom's coal supply was procured by the 'active coal spot market', which included firstly black women-owned suppliers, then small black suppliers, then large black suppliers, then black empowering suppliers and lastly, 'other' suppliers.

The following table indicates the amount of coal purchased, coal burnt and coal bought from BEE suppliers.

Eskom: Coal purchased, coal burnt, BEE purchases									
Year		2007	2006	2005	2004	2003	2002	2001	2000
Months		12 mths	12 mths	15 mths	12 mths	12 mths	12 mths	12 mths	12 mths
Coal burnt (Mt)	Actual	119,11	112,1	136,4	109,5	104,37	96,46	94,14	92,45
	Target	115,3	113,6	133,8	106,4	n/a	n/a	n/a	n/a
Coal bought (Mt)	Actual	117,4	111,7	137,8	112,7	104,9	92,8	89,1	n/a
	Target	120,1	125,3	135,0	106,8	n/a	89,3	n/a	n/a
BEE bought (Mt)		29,2	26,2	28,6	23,2	23,8	18,1	17,4	n/a

Source: Eskom annual reports 2002–2007.

Despite the fact that South Africa has 10% of the world's coal reserves, it seems the country's electricity supplier still cannot get it right. However, it has been said that Eskom is under pressure regarding coal prices as well as coal availability. The problem regarding coal availability partly has to do with the developments in China and India and the export of South Africa's coal to those countries, in addition to the approximate 56 million tonnes of coal exported to Europe. Also, the quality of coal required by importers is declining, making South Africa's current coal sources attractive as potential future sources to the export market.

The growth of South Africa's coal production is low and of great concern as it creates a serious supply risk to Eskom and South Africa. Eskom is under increasing risk with regard to securing future coal supplies from the local market, especially since coal production capacity has not kept up with increases in both local and international demand due to changes in the global market. If nothing is done about this, it is possible that South Africa may face an annual coal shortage of up to 100 million tons by 2017.

- The *third* interface between the business and its physical environment is the growing cost of urban pollution to the community in terms of a destroyed environment. The expense of fighting pollution and the laws that businesses have to obey in this regard are also important here. However, opportunities also present themselves in the form of recycling and new methods of manufacturing and packaging products in order to reduce pollution to the minimum.
- The *fourth* interface between the business and the physical environment is the field of environmentalism, which may be defined as *an organised movement of citizens and government institutions in defence of the natural* environment. Although the responsibility for a well-ordered ecology cannot be said to rest entirely with business organisations, they do make their mark on the ecology, for example by way of advertising boards, and packaging materials such as beer cans, soft-drink bottles and a variety of paper containers, all of which cause pollution, not to mention the marketing of products that are detrimental to people and the natural environment.

2.6.6   The politico-governmental environment

Management decisions are continually affected by a country's politics, especially the political pressures exerted by the government and its institutions in the business environment. As a component of the macro-environment, government affects the business environment and the business primarily as a regulating institution. By promulgating the enforcing legislation, it creates order by means of political measures, steering agricultural and economic policy in a particular direction. The policy of the South African government is based on maintaining the free-market system, private ownership, freedom of vocation and public condemnation of inequality, while the democratisation of the economy and public service is in full swing.

Hence the government intervenes in the local market on a large scale by means of the annual budget, taxation, import control or lack thereof, promotion of exports, import tariffs to protect certain industries against excessive foreign competition, price control for certain goods and services, and health regulation, as well as incentives and other measures to encourage development in a specific direction.

Black economic empowerment in South Africa

After South Africa achieved democracy in 1994, government introduced the legislation- and regulation-driven black economic empowerment (BEE). According to South Africa.info, BEE is a pragmatic growth strategy that aims to realise the country's full economic potential, not simply a moral initiative to redress the wrongs of the past.

➲

➲
The BEE policy instrument is aimed at broadening the economic base of the South Africa and stimulating economic growth and employment through equality and not inequality. It is government's way of actively promoting a more equitable distribution of wealth in a free-market context by supporting and favouring the economic empowerment of people from historically disadvantaged communities, particularly black people, women, youth, the disabled and rural communities.

Most companies in South Africa are required to follow the BEE policy. A company's empowerment progress is measured according to the sector-wide generic scorecard of the BEE Act of 2003 – a code of good practice. It measures progress in four areas:

- Direct empowerment through ownership and control of enterprises and assets.
- Management at senior level.
- Human resource development and employment equality.
- Indirect empowerment through:
  - preferential procurement;
  - enterprise development, and
  - corporate social investment (a residual and open-ended category).

Companies are required to apply the codes if they would like to tender for business, apply for licences and concessions, enter into public–private partnerships or buy state-owned assets.

The government also influences the market both internally and externally – internally through government investment and externally through its political policy, which may determine the acceptability or otherwise of South Africa for foreign investors. Whenever the government acts as a producer, as in the case of numerous government organisations, it competes with private business for labour, raw material and capital.

Privatisation, which occurs at a rather sluggish rate in South Africa, and which lacks credibility because of the growth rate in the public service workforce, can also create opportunities and threats. Since 1979, the British government has sold 40% of its assets at a value of some R40 billion to nine million private investors.

China is also moving in a direction of a free-market system and through privatisation has maintained a GDP and growth rate of 10% per annum for the past eight years. Russia is also moving in the direction of privatisation, which means that in the future, large consumer markets will probably be found in the East with China and India (both with a population of more than one billion) the emerging giant for the next number of years.

To an increasing extent, it is the task of management to study the numerous and often complex activities, legislation and measures of government as well as political trends to determine in good time their influence on the profitable survival of the business.

2.6.7 The international environment

While each of the above environmental factors to a greater or lesser extent influences the environment of each organisation, the situation is rendered even more complex with more opportunities and threats when an international dimension is added to each of the environmental factors. Businesses that operate internationally find themselves in a far more complex business environment because every country has its own unique environmental factors, with its own technology, culture, laws, politics, markets and competitiveness, which are different from those of other countries.

International and multinational organisations in particular are susceptible to all sorts of international currents.

The new economic order which is taking shape throughout the world is the increasing globalisation of the world economy. South African marketers should be able to find new opportunities in the fast changing environment. Globalisation has, however, entered a new phase, as explained in the information box below.

Globality – the new trend in the globalisation saga

A new trend has been identified by consultants of the Boston Consulting Group. This trend is called globality and is a counterreaction of the basic globalisation phenonenon that has been around for a number of decades.

The globalisation phenomenon was about European and the United States of America's multinationals such as Philips and McDonald's expanding into developing countries attracted primarily by low material and labour cost as well as expanding market demand.

In the globality phase the reverse situation is occurring, namely that organisations in rapidly developing economies such as Brazil, India, China and Russia are challenging multinationals not only in their countries but also in the home country of some of these multinationals. Companies such as Embraer (the fourth largest airplane manufacturer in the world from Brazil) is a case in point. It focuses on small business jets as well as regional jets that carry fewer than 120 passengers. Another example is the Tata group of India. It has entered the car market and is now exporting to various countries, such as South Africa.

➲

> ➲
> Three reasons for the success of these companies are as follows:
>
> - Their country of origin is a difficult place to do business in so they develop endurance which prepares them for easier access to developed countries.
> - They have global access to special skills like education, intellectual assets and innovation.
> - They have an insatiable hunger for success.

Nowadays, nations are also more dependent than ever on each other's technologies, economics, politics and raw material, so that the developments in these fields inevitably influence the decisions of management. Developing countries depend on technology imported from developed countries for their self-development. Inventions are excellent export products that offer opportunities, especially in the light of South Africa's expertise in mining, exploration of minerals, oil-from-coal technology and veterinary science.

The influence of international economic and political developments on local business, particularly in view of their closely interrelated nature, is multiple, and South African managers are only too aware of the extent to which international influences are exacerbated by domestic political problems.

2.6.8 The dynamic environment

In a free-market system, a business exists in a dynamic environment in which technological innovation, economic fluctuations, changing communities and life-styles as well as political change continually alter the environment and ultimately affect it.

An insight into and understanding of trends and events in the environment and an ability to foresee the implications thereof for decision making are becoming increasingly important for management since past experience in a rapidly changing environment is often of little help in solving new problems that confront management, and mere expansion of issues that largely determine the direction in which the business will develop are also necessary for decision making in order to maximise profitability. This knowledge requires environmental scanning that enables management to identify threats and demands in the environment timeously and, wherever possible, to turn them into opportunities.

2.7 Methods of environmental scanning

The degree to which the environment influences the management of a business depends largely on the type of business and the objectives it intends achieving. Moreover, environmental influences differ from one management function to the next and even at different levels of management in an organisation. As such, the importance, scope and method of environmental scanning – that is, the process dealing with the measurement, projection and evaluation of change in the different environmental variables – differs from one business to the next.

The importance of environmental scanning is clear from the following points:

- The environment is continually changing, so that purposeful scanning by management is necessary to keep abreast of change.
- Scanning is necessary to determine which factors in the environment pose a threat to the business's present goals and strategy.
- Scanning is also necessary to determine which factors in the environment present opportunities for the more effective attainment of goals by modifying present strategy.
- Organisations that scan the environment systematically are more successful than those that do not.

The scope of environmental scanning is determined by the following factors:

- The nature of the environment within which the organisation operates and the demands made by the environment on the business. The more unstable the environment and the more sensitive the business is to change, the more comprehensive the scanning has to be. Increasing instability usually means greater risk for the business.
- Managers nowadays should constantly bear in mind the basic relationships between the business and its environment. The importance or otherwise of any one or more of these relationships for management will affect the scope of environmental scanning.
- The source and scope of change will also influence the extent of meaningful environmental scanning. The impact of change is rarely so compartmentalised that it influences only one or two areas of an organisation. Change has an interactive and dynamic effect on various facets of the business.

The method of environmental scanning is a much-debated subject, and the following possible approaches can be followed:

- The most elementary basis for environmental scanning is *to keep abreast of the relevant secondary or published information obtainable from a vast wealth of sources,* such as the media, own data, professional publications, financial journals, statistics, associates in other organisations, banks, research institutions and even employees. Such information may be added to the management information system of the organisation.
- A more advanced basis for scanning would be the *addition of primary information or special studies on particular aspects of the environment.* Such studies can be carried out by members or the organisation's own staff, or by outside consultants.

- A far more advanced basis is the *establishment of a unit within the organisation which scans a wide range of environmental factors and makes forecasts about specific variables*. Examples here are the economic predictions made by economists using a number of models, market and competition assessments by market researchers, and technological predictions by industrial analysts. Such a scanning unit is usually located in the planning department of top management, and has its own staff.

The question that now arises is how this collected environmental information can be brought to the attention of the appropriate manager. There are many different opinions about this, the most popular approach being that environmental information forms the basis of strategic planning undertaken by top management.

Summary

The business and the community it serves are not self-sufficient and closed entities but depend on each other for survival. Together they form a complex, dynamic business or marketing environment in which changes in the environmental variables continually determine the prosperity or otherwise of the business. Since these variables are more often than not beyond the control of the organisation, it is the task of management to adapt constantly to change. Sometimes management operates proactively – in other words, takes the lead and anticipates events, thereby augmenting change.

Knowledge of a changing environment through sustained environmental scanning is a prerequisite for taking advantage of opportunities and averting threats. Environmental scanning is discussed in chapter 3, which deals with marketing research.

References

1. Based on Du Toit, GS, Erasmus, BJ & Strydom, JW. 2007. *Introduction to business management*, 7th ed. Cape Town: Oxford, ch 4.
2. Scher, M. 2007. *Baby boomers ignored by South African marketers.* [Online] Available from: http://www.bizcommunity.com/Print.aspx?l=196&c=11&ci=27446 (accessed: 19 August 2008).
3. Pearce, JA & Robinson, RB. 1988. *Formulation and implementation of competitive strategy.* Homewood, III; Richard D Irwin Inc, p 202.
4. Vasconcellos e Sá, J. 1988. The impact of key success factors on company performance. *Long-range Planning 21*, pp 56–64.
5. Bureau of Market Research, Unisa. 2007. *Population and household projections for South Africa by province and population group*, 2001–2021, no. 364, p 2.
6. Kotler, P. 1997. *Marketing management: Analysis, planning, implementation and control.* Englewood Cliffs, NJ: Prentice Hall, p 229.

7. Goldstuck, A. 2008. *State of online media in SA*. [Online] Available from: http://www.slideshare.net/classicevents/state-of-online-media-in-south-africa-arthur-goldstuck-worldwideworx-presentation/
    Salient Communications. 2008. *Kulula strengthens online reach with Clicks2Customers*. [Online] Available from: http://www.itweb.co.za/sections/internet/2008/0803310802.asp?A=ITR&S=Retail%2
    Economist Intelligence Unit. 2007. Overview of e-commerce in South Africa, e-commerce: Forms of e-commerce. [Online] Available from: http://www.ibls.com/internet_law_news_portal_view.aspx?s=sa&id=1098

8. Kotler, P & Keller, KL. 2007. *A framework for marketing management*, 3rd ed. Upper Saddle River, NJ: Pearson Prentice Hall, p 59.

9. Adapted from: Knowledge @ Wharton. 6 August 2008. *A precarious road: How retailers can navigate inflation's hazards*. Available from: http://knowledge.wharton.upenn.edu/article.cfn?articleid=2008 (accessed: 7 August 2008).

10. Fin24. [Online] Available from: http://www.fin24.com/articles/default/display_article.aspx?Nav=ns&ArticleID=1518-25_2370733 (accessed: 7 August 2008).

11. Ryan, B. 2008. *Eskom faces competition for coal supplies*. [Online] Available from: http://www.miningmx.com/energy/671444.htm
    Reuters. 2008. *FACTBOX-Coal export problems in key areas create shortage*. [Online] Available from: http://uk.reuters.com/article/oilRpt/idUKL29398920080129?pageNumber=4&virtualBrandChannel=0&sp=true
    In the news. 2008. *What caused the Eskom crisis?* [Online] Available from: http://www.inthenews.co.za/2008/07/15/what-caused-the-eskom-crisis/
    Myburgh, J. 2008. *Eskom: The real cause of the crisis*. [Online] Available from: http://www.politicsweb.co.za/politicsweb/view/politicsweb/en/page71627?oid=85789&sn=Detail
    Yelland, C. 2008. *The role of coal in the generation capacity crisis in South Africa*. [Online] Available from: http://www.eepublishers.co.za/print.php?sid=12054&DC100SID=575abbaa7e6bdc0529116c39e632a3af

12. South Africa.info. 2008. *Black economic empowerment*. [Online] Available from: http://www.southafrica.info/business/trends/empowerment/bee.htm

13. Knowledge @ Wharton. 2008. *Whether you agree with globalilty or disagree, don't ignore*. [Online] Available from http://knowledge.wharton.upenn.edu/article.cfm?articleid=2037 (accessed: 21 August 2008).

Marketing research

3.1 Introduction

In order to be successful and to adapt to the ever-changing market environment, a company needs reliable and relevant information to be able to aid decision making. The worst thing that can happen to a company is to make decisions based on information that is incorrect or not relevant. This may lead to money and other resources being wasted. The ability of a company to gather usable information ensures that it remains competitive not only locally but also internationally. In fact, information is the engine that drives today's global marketplace. Companies succeed by knowing what consumers want, and when and where they want it – and by knowing what competing companies are doing about it. A sophisticated database of marketing information is a vital component in the strategy of cutting-edge companies that pull ahead and stay ahead in the race for customers.

Large and small companies such as Standard Bank, ABSA, Pep Stores, Iliad, Aca Joe and others rely on information from their markets in order to survive. In order to be in business for as long as they have, they have 'heard' the consumers' wants and needs, and conceived a product (or service), and a price, promotion and distribution method that satisfied them.

Mercedes-Benz, for example, monitors luxury car market trends around the world in order to stay competitive. The company relies on consumer research and marketing information from various sources to keep on top of what product benefits, features and services customers all over the world desire and will accept. Mercedes-Benz stays out in front of the highly competitive market by finding out what it takes to tempt consumers into spending up to R2 million for their high-quality driving machines.

It is not always difficult to obtain information but it is crucial for a company that the correct information is obtained. Some information regarding a company's consumers and conditions in the marketplace is easy to obtain, while some information requires the company to conduct in-depth research to make informed marketing decisions. By monitoring daily customer activity, for example, marketing managers can respond very quickly to changes in consumers' needs and buying patterns that could mean the difference between the success and failure of marketing plans.

Marketing researchers are increasingly making use of the Internet for a variety of marketing research purposes. The range of information that is available either for free or at a relatively low cost is staggering and is growing at an alarming rate. Most sources of secondary data are available online and can be downloaded at anytime, enquiries can be handled fast, and even primary research in a global market can be conducted fairly quickly and cost effectively.

In this chapter, we look at the kinds of information marketers need and how they gather and use that information to develop marketing strategies that make a difference. In this discussion, we focus on the marketing information system, marketing research, and market potential and sales forecasting.

3.2 The role of marketing research in decision making

3.2.1 *The value of marketing information*

Marketing research can be defined as *the process of gathering and analysing data based on solving a problem or exploiting an opportunity and then reporting information on this opportunity or problem in such a way that marketing management can utilise it in its decision making.*

The main role of marketing research is to provide information that facilitates marketing decisions.[1] We know that marketing is *the performance of all activities necessary for the conception, pricing, promotion and distribution of ideas, goods and services to create exchanges that satisfy individual and organisational objectives.* The potential for exchange exists when there are at least two parties and each has something of potential value to the other. Now the question arises as to how marketing managers attempt to stimulate exchange. They follow the 'right' principle: they attempt to get the right goods and services to the right people at the right place at the right time at the right price using the right promotion techniques. In order to make the 'right' decisions, management must have timely decision-making information, and marketing research is a primary channel for providing it.

In terms of the consumer orientation principle of the marketing concept, companies strive to identify the group of people most likely to buy their product (the target market) and produce goods or services that will meet the needs of the target customers most effectively. But how does a company know what consumers' needs and wants are? Obviously marketers must have information about consumers' needs and wants if they are truly to endorse the marketing concept. Identifying target market needs and market opportunities is the task of marketing research.

Quality and customer satisfaction have become the key competitive weapons of the early 21st century.[2] Few organisations will prosper in today's environment without a focus on quality and customer satisfaction. The key to quality and customer satisfaction is marketing research; it is the mechanism that enables companies to determine the type and forms of quality that are important to the target market. Customer satisfaction and quality lead to customer retention. The ability to retain customers is based upon an intimate understanding of their needs. This knowledge comes primarily from marketing research.

Customer service at Toyota

Toyota SA realised in the mid-1980s that a shift in focus was needed to satisfy the customers – the concept of customer satisfaction had to be managed and measured. By shifting the focus and educating dealers to see through the customer's eyes, Toyota tried to improve the service experience of customers. The Toyota Touch programme relies heavily on marketing research in the form of regular surveys. It was implemented in the mid-1980 and included:

- establishing and maintaining a customer-oriented culture;
- developing an obsession among staff at Toyota with customers and the satisfaction of their needs; and
- developing a competitive advantage in terms of customer satisfaction by aiming for a top rating in the SA motor industry.

Toyota succeeded in establishing a competitive advantage in terms of customer service. Its overall rating by customers has increased every year. In the 1998 *Sunday Times*/Markinor Top Brands survey, Toyota was rated as one of the top ten brands in South Africa, as well as the fifth most admired company in South Africa.

Marketing research is also used in decision making about the marketing mix, keeping abreast of changes in the marketing environment, and identifying and defining marketing opportunities and problems in an effort to monitor marketing performance and to improve understanding of the marketing process.

British Airways: Understanding customer needs

British Airways research found that most first-class passengers simply wanted to sleep. BA now gives business-class passengers the option of dinner on the ground before takeoff in the first-class lounge. Once on board, they can slip into BA pajamas, put their heads on real pillows, slip under blankets, and then enjoy an interruption-free flight.

3.2.2 Marketing research and the marketing mix

Marketers must also implement plans, called marketing strategies, that actually satisfy consumers' wants and needs. Within the marketing department, a marketing mix, based on the marketing concept, must be created. This mix is the unique blend of the four Ps (product, price, promotion and place) designed to reach a specific group of consumers (target market).[3] What combination of the four Ps will best take advantage of an existing marketing opportunity? This may sound simple, but consider some of the questions that confront marketing managers as they design marketing strategies:

Questions to answer when designing marketing strategies

- Who is the market?
- How do we segment the market?
- What are the wants and needs of each segment?
- How do we measure the size of each market segment?
- Who are our competitors, and how are they meeting the wants and needs of each segment?
- Which segment(s) should we target?
- Which model of a proposed product will best suit the target market?
- What is the best price?
- Which promotional method will be the most efficient?
- How should we distribute the product/service?

These questions must be answered. Therefore, marketing managers need objective, accurate and current information in order to develop marketing strategies that will work. Sears, the well-known US retailer, for example, relies heavily on consumer research to obtain this information.

3.2.3 Marketing research and the macro-marketing environment

Marketers operate in a turbulent, ever-evolving environment and need the right information to implement an effective marketing strategy as any change may alter the appeal of a marketing strategy to consumers. As such, marketers' needs for information are never ending. Information about the social and cultural environment, economic environment, political environment and technological environment is of particular importance to marketing management in its decision making.

In the deteriorating world economic climate since 2008, information pertaining to these environments and its impact on the company and its customers has become extremely important. Changes taking place in the social and cultural environment, for instance, must be monitored on a continuous basis. For example, as the population ages, some companies are developing or redesigning products and services to cater for the older market. Computer keyboards have been developed with large-print key-top labels, making it easier for older people with deteriorating eyesight to use them more easily. Information on the effect of economic factors will also affect marketing decisions. Owing to the recession in 2009 many companies have abandoned their more expensive ranges of products for more economical products which are affordable to their customers. Marketers use marketing research to keep abreast of these changes.

The South African social environment[4]

South African business is affected by the following changes in the social environment:

- The narrowing gap in the standards of living between black and white consumers, and the rise in literacy among black people.
- The increasing number of single-parent families.
- The black age structure that reflects a much more youthful population, largely urbanised – this impacts on demand and consumption patterns.
- Growing urbanisation which has resulted, for example, in the advent of the spaza store.
- The changing role of women in our society.

The South African economic environment[5]

Important factors in the economic environment which impact on business are as follows:

- The inflation rate (about 8% in June 2009) results in high prices and changes in consumer spending.
- In 2008 the world entered a period of recession, signifying increasing unemployment, decreasing purchases and a resultant decline in profits.
- The white household income is six times that of black households.
- Black households have a major share of the market for many individual products such as washing materials, clothing, footwear, cigarettes and tobacco.
- Violence discourages foreign investment and tourism.

➲

- The political environment, by way of the government, influences society indirectly via its influence on the economy and technology, The political environment thus influences marketing strategy. The fact that cigarette advertising has been banned from being advertised on television and radio, for sponsorships, and in all media has posed serious challenges for the manufacturers of these products, who have to rethink their entire marketing strategy in view of these changes. Pressure is also exerted on companies to implement affirmative action programmes. Research is required to formulate a response to these changes.

- *Technological environment.* The rate of change in the technological environment is unprecedented in the history of the world. The popularity of the World Wide Web has spurred demand for digital cameras, particularly for online images. To be competitive, all companies must keep abreast of information about technological changes that may impact their productivity and, in some instances, their ability to survive and remain competitive.

The computer in direct marketing

The computer has been the driving force behind the growing importance of direct marketing by means of extensive databases which enable it to become focused and individual. The decreasing cost of computer technology makes it more and more affordable to advertisers. The introduction of direct response television (telemarketing), with the advent of toll-free numbers, permits immediate response.

Marketers must therefore develop and implement strategies, and those strategies must constantly be revised as required by changing environments. This means marketers constantly need information provided by marketing research. Without this, it is difficult, if not impossible, for management to make sound decisions or to implement the marketing concept properly.

3.2.4 *Marketing research identifies and defines marketing opportunities and problems*

To identify and define marketing opportunities means to define those wants and needs in the market that are not being met by the competition. Opportunities and problems are everywhere, but decision makers need information to help identify and define them adequately. This information is acquired by way of conducting continuous research.

> **Identifying marketing opportunities by means of research**
>
> Many fast-food companies such as McDonald's and KFC have discovered opportunities arising from consumers' increasing concerns about health, weight and diet, and have introduced new foods to the market that are low in cholesterol, fat, sodium and sugar (e.g. salads). McDonald's and KFC research has revealed that there is an opportunity in the market for 'intelligent cuisine'.
>
> People have also become more concerned about environmental hazards and the problem with waste in landfill sites. McDonald's took advantage of this opportunity by building their outlets with recyclable materials.

3.2.5 *Marketing research monitors marketing performance*

Monitoring marketing strategies once they are implemented is a way of maintaining control over the success of a new product or service. Any control system requires feedback of information to management, which is what marketing research does, allowing a comparison between actual performance and desired performance standards.

3.2.6 *Marketing research improves understanding of the marketing process*

Marketing research conducted to expand basic knowledge of marketing is known as *basic research*. Typical of such research would be attempts to define and classify certain marketing phenomena and to determine optimum methods for carrying out marketing activities, for example studies to determine optimum returns on promotional expenditures or the operating characteristics of the most profitable firms within an industry.

Basic research thus attempts to expand the frontiers of knowledge and is not aimed at a specific pragmatic problem. Basic research hopes to provide further confirmation for an existing theory or to learn more about a concept. For example, basic research might test a hypothesis on high-involvement decision making or consumer information processing. In the long run, basic research helps us to understand more about the world in which we live.

Most marketing research is conducted to improve understanding of the marketplace, for example to find out why a strategy failed or to reduce uncertainty in management decision making. All research conducted for such purposes is called *applied research*. For example, should the price of frozen dinners be raised by 40 cents? What name should Nissan select for the new car? Which advertisement has the highest level of recall: A or B?

Marketing research is not the only source of information available to decision makers. It is also supplied by the various components of the marketing information system (MIS) of which marketing research is one.

3.3 The marketing information system (MIS)

3.3.1 Information management

Data and information are not the same. Information is data that has been converted into a useful form for decision making – for solving a problem. It is relevant, timely, accurate and cost effective, and it reduces risk in decision making. Marketers face an immense volume of raw data generated internally and externally. If this data is to be useful, the data flow must be managed.

Marketers must consider the cost of collecting and converting data into information when specifying their informational needs. Seldom will they have all the information they want. Thus the cost of additional information must be weighed against its value for planning, implementing and controlling marketing operations.

The company's sales force should also be trained in intelligence gathering. Its close contact with the market can make it a useful data source for manufacturers, retailers and wholesalers. Too often, however, salespeople are trained only in selling techniques. Many companies develop an MIS to gather, sort, analyse, store and distribute relevant and timely marketing information to managers continuously.

The MIS is part of a company's overall information network that integrates electronic records from all the company's functional areas. The purpose of an MIS is to help marketing managers make better decisions. It guides the planning process and leads to meaningful marketing goals and objectives. Having the right information available at the right time also enables managers to make on-the-spot decisions when unforeseen events threaten to derail the marketing plan.

We can now define an MIS as a *system for generating and managing a flow of information for marketing decision making*.

3.3.2 Components of a marketing information system

Marketing information systems differ according to the type of company and industry. A small company usually has a simple MIS and a large company has an extensive one. A simple MIS, as illustrated in figure 3.1, consists of two data components: routine data and special purpose data.[6]

For a local independent retailer, the routine data component would include, for example, routine information from internal sources such as sales, stocks, debtors and creditors. From external sources, information such as local population growth, competitive activities and trade association statistics can be collected on a regular basis. The special-purpose component includes marketing research, for example where a retailer engages a marketing research organisation to determine the feasibility of a particular retail space in a new shopping centre (external marketing research). The retailer conducting certain research projects independently, for example a survey among existing customers to determine their degree of satisfaction with its services, constitutes internal marketing research (launched from internal sources).

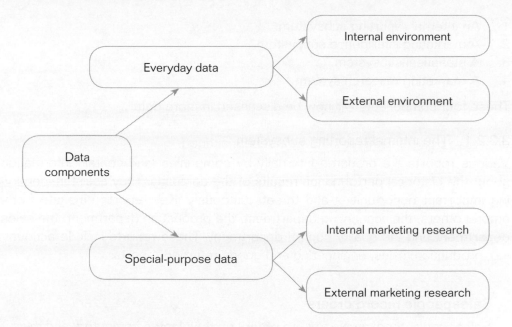

Figure 3.1 A simple marketing information system

Source: Adapted from Martins, JH, Loubser, M & Van Wyk, H de J in Cant, MC (Ed). 2004. *Essentials of marketing*, 2nd ed. Cape Town: Juta, p 78.

Larger companies that have the necessary resources usually operate an extensive MIS. The major components of this and the interaction among its components are indicated in figure 3.2.[7]

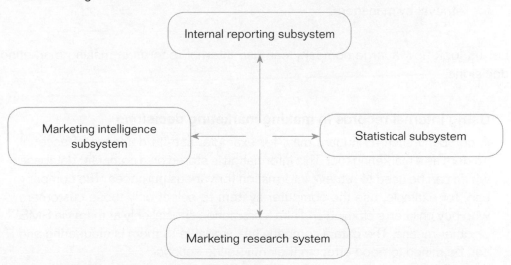

Figure 3.2 An extensive marketing information system

Source: Adapted from Marx, S & Van der Walt, A in Cant, MC (Ed). 2004. *Essentials of marketing*, 2nd ed. Cape Town: Juta, p 79.

The four major components of an extensive marketing information system, as indicated in figure 3.2 are:

1. An internal reporting subsystem.
2. A marketing intelligence subsystem.
3. A statistical subsystem.
4. A marketing research system.

These four components will now be discussed in more detail.

3.3.2.1 The internal reporting subsystem

Various reports are prepared internally by companies, and contain information about the historical performance results of the company. They assist in identifying important opportunities and threats timeously. Key reports emanate from, among others, the accounting department, the production department, the sales department and the quality control department. These reports include accounting, production, sales, engineering and goods returned reports.

Salespeople record orders

Salespeople, for example, record orders on their laptop computers and this information is sent via modem to the company headquarters, which notifies the warehouse to expedite delivery. The information recorded during this process – customer's name, location, goods ordered, prices, delivery location, method of delivery, date, and so on – becomes the information ingredients in the internal reports system. The internal reporting subsystem ensures that information generated is recorded, stored and made available for retrieval by managers.

Let us look how a large company can use internal records in making marketing decisions.

Using internal records in making marketing decisions

A company such as Edgars may, for example, use its database of account holders as a marketing tool. This information is stored on a computer database which can be used to retrieve information for various purposes. The company can, for example, use the computer system to select only those customers who buy children's clothing and aim a promotion special only at them via SMS or other means. The data a company has available to them is staggering and can be mined to good effect in their marketing actions.

3.3.2.2 The marketing intelligence subsystem

This subsystem consists of procedures and sources whereby management obtains information concerning current and relevant occurrences in the marketing environment.

Whereas an internal reporting system focuses on *results,* the intelligence system focuses on *happenings* in the marketing environment. The marketing intelligence subsystem includes both informal and formal information-gathering procedures. *Informal information-gathering procedures* involve such activities as scanning newspapers, magazines and trade publications. *Formal information-gathering activities* may be conducted by staff members who are assigned the specific task of looking for anything that seems pertinent to the company or industry. They then edit and disseminate this information to the appropriate members of the company.

Purchasing information

Some companies find it advantageous to purchase information from specialist organisations on a regular basis. In South Africa, International Business Information Systems (IBIS), which has an association with the internationally reputable ACNielsen, is well known for the retail audits which it regularly conducts. This information includes aspects such as market share, retail prices, inventory levels and marketing communications.

3.3.2.3 The statistical subsystem

The statistical subsystem is a composition of a statistical database and the application of advanced statistical procedures and techniques. The purpose of this system is to create projections, scenarios and models which provide a better grasp of the alternatives for decision making. Decision making always takes place in conditions of risk and uncertainty. With this subsystem, an attempt is made to quantify the probable results of various possible actions of marketing management.

A variety of statistical data series is stored and regularly updated in the statistical subsystem. This serves as a basis for the application of statistical techniques (with multiple variables), forecasting techniques and the creation of models. These models allow companies to ask 'what if' questions.

Answers to these questions are then immediately available for decision making. A model can, for example, illustrate the probable effect of a change in consumer price on consumer behaviour.

3.3.2.4 The marketing research subsystem

The marketing research subsystem gathers information not collected by the other MIS component subsystems. Marketing research studies are conducted for a *specific* situation facing the company. It is unlikely that other components of MIS have generated the *particular* information needed for the *specific* situation. This is why people in the industry sometimes refer to marketing research studies as ad hoc studies. 'Ad hoc' is a Latin term meaning 'with respect to a specific purpose'.

Marketing research projects, unlike the other components of the MIS, are not continuous – they have a beginning and an end. This is why marketing research studies are sometimes referred to as 'projects'.

Marketing research problems

- A company that suspects a change in consumer preferences would investigate this problem by means of a marketing research project.
- A bank may wish to measure its competitiveness. Marketing research is then conducted.
- A company may want to develop target customer profiles. Marketing research is then employed.
- An advertising agency may need to know more about the scheduling of advertisements and can use marketing research to solve this problem.
- A manufacturer of cosmetics may need to know which packaging would be the most acceptable and conducts marketing research among customers to accomplish this.

We will now focus on one component of the MIS, namely marketing research.

3.4 Marketing research

Some of marketing management's most important decisions rely on information gathered by research that specifically addresses the decision maker's concerns.

Many decisions require information

- Sales personnel rely on research to provide them with feedback on sales performance or to identify likely purchasers.
- Media planners need information to determine which specific magazines or television shows will most likely be seen by a market segment.
- Advertising executives need feedback to 'flesh out' the needs and wants of target consumers.
- Brand managers need to determine how their product is perceived in the marketplace, especially relative to other competing brands.

Some marketers conduct limited, low-cost research projects by searching the MIS database and gathering the required information. More typically, the marketer has a problem that requires very specific information and must rely on marketing research to gather data systematically.

Large companies like Unilever have extensive marketing research capabilities to conduct their own research. Depending on the information required and the complexity of the research problem, companies such as ACNielsen, Markinor and BMR (Unisa) may be hired to conduct all or part of the research.

Finding marketing research companies on the Internet

The Internet is a powerful tool for identifying research companies that provide particular types of services and for conducting a preliminary review of these companies. Most research companies' sites are e-mail enabled. Therefore, after research buyers have identified likely candidates through preliminary research and evaluation, they can send an e-mail to these organisations, requesting additional information. A few companies even have RFP (requests for proposal) forms on their sites which permit the research buyer to submit an RFP via e-mail. In this way, one can review the services offered by marketing research companies.

3.4.1 Steps in the marketing research process

The marketing research process is a series of carefully thought-out steps designed to attain a specific objective. This section looks at the different steps in the marketing research process.

There are various reasons why marketing research is undertaken. Consider the following:

Reasons why marketing research needs to be conducted

- Top management delegates the marketing management to investigate the possibility of an attractive marketing opportunity.
- Marketing management must develop a marketing strategy for a new product.
- There is a decline in demand for the company's products, and marketing management is instructed to determine the cause and recommend remedial action.

As we can see, each of these reasons is in some way unique, and the procedures followed in the research process of each will vary to some extent. For example, the research process in the case of an investigation into a decline in sales will differ from an investigation into the development of a marketing strategy for a new product.

Although the research processes or procedures may differ for different types of problems or opportunities, a marketing research investigation consists of two parts: a *preliminary* marketing investigation and a *formal* marketing investigation. Both investigations may need to be conducted, but if the problem is solved during the preliminary investigation, a formal investigation will not be required. However, for the formal investigation to be conducted satisfactorily, there needs to be a preliminary investigation.

The marketing research process may be viewed as a number of consecutive steps undertaken to obtain the required marketing information. Although authors differ on the number of stages involved in the research process, they all agree that some basic stages should be included. Figure 3.3 reflects a logical 11-step approach to the marketing research process, which is discussed in detail below.[8]

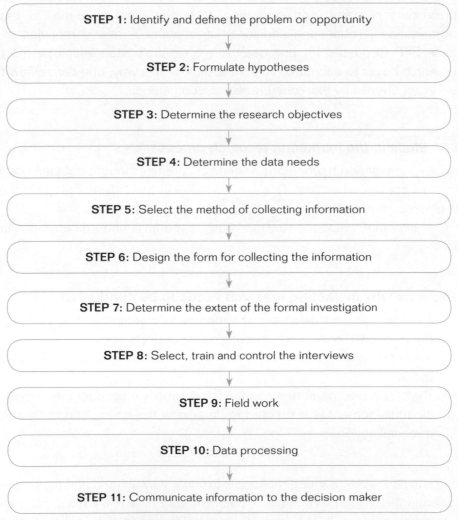

STEP 1: Identify and define the problem or opportunity

STEP 2: Formulate hypotheses

STEP 3: Determine the research objectives

STEP 4: Determine the data needs

STEP 5: Select the method of collecting information

STEP 6: Design the form for collecting the information

STEP 7: Determine the extent of the formal investigation

STEP 8: Select, train and control the interviews

STEP 9: Field work

STEP 10: Data processing

STEP 11: Communicate information to the decision maker

Figure 3.3 Steps in the marketing research process

Source: Cooper, DR & Schindler, PS. 2006. *Business research methods*, 9th ed. New York, NY: McGraw-Hill.

3.4.1.1   The preliminary marketing investigation

Step 1: Identify and define the problem or opportunity

This first step of the marketing research process entails a clear definition of the nature and extent of the problem or opportunity. Often there is only a vague feeling that 'something is wrong' and management has at its disposal contradictory pieces of information, reports, opinions and symptoms such as a decline in sales figures. In order to take appropriate action, it is essential to know more about the problem or opportunity. Thus, the real nature and extent of the problem should be determined. For example, if a decline in sales of a company's products has been discovered, further investigation (by means of small-scale research) may reveal that the decline is restricted to a particular area, for example Pretoria.

Typical problems (or opportunities) that may require a marketing research investigation are the following:

Problems (or opportunities) that must be investigated

- Which of two package designs best conveys the desired image for the product?
- More general information for a planning decision is required.
- A brand manager who is planning to changes packaging may want to know the features of a package that may create interest in consumers.
- Owing to changes that occur in the company's external environment that are not controlled by the company, a marketing manager is faced with the questions: 'Should we change the existing marketing strategy and, if so, how?'
- Marketing research may be needed to evaluate the marketing mix alternatives.
- Marketing research may be needed to establish and evaluate new market opportunities.

Once a problem has been identified, the marketing researcher is approached. The first responsibility of the researcher, whether from internal staff or an outside consulting company, is to work with the marketing manager to define precisely the problem. Proper definition of a problem also provides guidance and direction for the entire process.

In an attempt to define the exact nature of the problem or opportunity and to gain a better understanding of the environment within which the problem has occurred, it may be necessary to conduct small-scale research.

Small-scale research at Toyota

About ten years ago, Toyota launched its minibus, the Venture, which has proved to be one of the most successful new motor vehicle products in decades. Toyota needs to understand the changing needs and wishes of the target market to maintain its market share. The problem in this case is that Toyota must deliver exceptional value to the target customer to maintain and build market share and profits.

In order to identify and define the problem, Toyota researchers, in conducting small-scale research, may act as follows:

- Review secondary data on several existing studies and articles on driving trends.
- Benchmark with competing dealers by visiting them to determine which features they are promoting and their selling techniques.
- A small-scale survey of consumers might be developed along with interviews of company executives.
- Small groups (consumer audits) may be consulted to discuss driving habits.
- Experts could be consulted. For example, the research could seek out publishers of car magazines and research at the Department of Transport (published data).

The marketing researcher now possesses information on the nature and extent of the problem or opportunity. The next step is to formulate hypotheses that need to be investigated.

Step 2: Formulate hypotheses

In this step, specific factors which can be identified as influencing factors or the causes of the problem or opportunity are identified. From this group of factors, some are selected which are considered important enough to be further investigated. These are called *hypotheses*. Hypotheses can thus be seen as tentative solutions or actions for the problem or opportunity. A hypothesis is a theory that has to be tested or proved to confirm the assumptions.

For example, let us assume that a company experiences a decline in sales. There are many factors or variables which may be the cause of this.

If all these possible causes need to be investigated, several research projects would have to be undertaken. Further investigation, however, may reveal that only one of the possible causes should be investigated, for example a change in consumer preferences. This will then be translated into a hypothesis for further investigation.

Possible causes of a decline in sales

- Certain actions by competitors, for example price discounting.
- A change in consumer preferences.
- The employment of an inefficient marketing mix strategy.
- A combination of all these variables.

One or more of these may be identified as the possible cause(s) of the decline in sales; in other words, one of these statements may be termed the *hypothesis.*

Confirming or rejecting the hypotheses is a crucial phase of the research project. During this process, new information may come to light and it may be deemed necessary to redefine certain problems (or hypotheses). The following example illustrates how a problem can be redefined:[9]

Redefinition of a problem

The sales manager of a local potato crisp manufacturer notices that sales are declining, and interprets the problem as ineffective advertising (hypothesis).

The researcher is therefore asked to investigate the effectiveness of the company's advertising. In talking to salespeople, wholesalers and retailers of the company's products, however, the researcher discovers that the support for the product began to decline when a rival company introduced a new product that gave them a larger margin on sales. Retailers are therefore making more profit by selling the rival's product.

This gives the researcher a new perspective on the problem. An investigation of advertising effectiveness will not help solve the problem. This hypothesis must then be rejected and redefined as *competitive pricing and profit margin tactics.*

Step 3: Determine the research objectives

Once the problem has been identified and clearly defined, and hypotheses have been formulated, the researcher can determine the objectives of the research project. These objectives are stated in terms of the precise information necessary and desired to solve the marketing problem. The objectives must relate directly to the hypotheses formulated during step two. In fact, the hypotheses become the research objectives. For example:

H1: The competitive pricing and profit margin tactics have a negative effect on company profit.

Objective: To determine whether the competitive pricing and profit margins tactics have a negative effect on company profit.

Research objectives

A decline in sales in one of the company's products has been established (in other words, the symptom). The problem has been identified and defined, and subsequently one hypothesis has been formulated, namely that *consumer preferences have changed*. The research objective in this case could be *to investigate competitive pricing and profit margin tactics*.

Well-formulated objectives serve as a road map in developing the research project. They also serve as a standard which enables managers to evaluate the quality and value of the work.

Were the objectives met and do the recommendations flow logically from the objectives and the research findings? Objectives must be as specific and unambiguous as possible. Putting the objectives in writing avoids the problem of wondering whether the information that has been received is, in fact, what is required.

In general, a research investigation will have one of four basic objectives:

1. To explore.
2. To describe.
3. To test hypotheses (causal research).
4. To predict.

These four objectives will now be described in more detail.

- *To explore.* The primary objective of exploratory research is to provide insights into and an understanding of the problem confronting the researcher (as explained earlier). Once the problem has been clearly defined, exploratory research can be useful in identifying alternative courses of action. Researchers conduct exploratory research when they need more information about the problem, when tentative hypotheses need to be formulated more specifically, or when new hypotheses are required.[10] Because exploratory research is aimed at gaining additional information about a topic and generating possible hypotheses to test, it is described as informal research.

Examples of exploratory research

- Visiting the library to read published secondary data.
- Asking customers and salespeople their opinions about a company and its products, services and prices.
- Simply observing everyday company practices.

The researcher investigates whatever sources he or she desires to the extent that he or she feels is necessary in order to gain a good understanding of the problem.

- *To describe.* Descriptive research is necessary when knowledge about a particular market or marketing aspect is vague. It includes research designed to provide answers to questions regarding the who, what, when, where and how of a topic. For example, an enterprise that is considering entering the hospitality industry may have identified the conference market as one of their target markets. This market, however, needs further clarification and must be described more clearly. Descriptive research may also be necessary where the nature of the competition in a particular industry is vague. Soft-drink marketers also use this type of research to describe the characteristics and wants of different market segments.
- *To test hypotheses (causal research).* If the objective is to test hypotheses about the relationship between an independent and a dependent variable, the researcher engages in causal research. Causal research would be used in the following example:

Independent and dependent variables in causal research

What would happen to sales if prices were reduced? Price is the independent variable – that is, the factor being manipulated. The sales level is the dependent variable that will be affected when the independent variable (price) is changed (price is reduced).

What would happen to customer awareness of the product if advertising were to be increased? Advertising is the independent variable, while awareness is the dependent variable that will be affected when the independent variable (advertising) is changed (advertising increased).

Causal research is therefore used to obtain evidence of cause-and-effect relationships. It attempts to determine the extent to which changes in the one variable cause changes in another.

Causal research versus descriptive research

Descriptive research may suggest that a price reduction is associated with increased sales of a product, but it does not definitely suggest that a decrease in price was the actual *cause* of the sales increase. Sales may have increased because of other factors, such as an increase in customer buying power or a decline in competitors' marketing efforts.

Causal research, on the other hand, tries to show either that the price cut (independent variable) is the cause of increased sales (dependent variable) or that the price cut is not the cause of increased sales. This requires the researcher to keep all factors other than price and sales constant – at best, a difficult task.

- *To predict.* Predictive research is conducted to forecast future values, for example sales income, market share and retail orders. Political pollsters use predictive research to forecast how many people will vote for a particular candidate in an upcoming election. Businesses engage in sales forecasting to predict sales of the products during a specific time period, for example a financial year.

Step 4: Determine the data needs

In this step, the research objectives must be translated into specific data needs. This means determining what information is required and from which sources it can be obtained in order to test the hypotheses so that the problem can be solved. For example:

Specific data needs: The South African Police Service (SAPS)

Suppose the SAPS wants to establish what steps it can take to improve the quality of recruits. The information necessary to satisfy this research objective might include:

- A detailed description of recruiting incentives currently being offered by the SAPS.
- Young people's attitudes toward existing recruiting incentives offered by the SAPS.
- The demographic and lifestyle characteristics of current police enlistees who are high achievers.
- A detailed description of recruiting activities currently in use at recruiting centres.
- A forecast of unemployment rates for the next decade.

In determining the type of data needed, the problem (step 1), the hypotheses (step 2) and the objectives (step 3) must be considered. Specific data will be needed in order to confirm or reject each hypothesis that has been formulated.

Researchers distinguish between secondary and primary data. *Secondary data* is data that was previously collected by people either inside or outside the company to meet their needs. If it can assist in solving the problem – that is, to confirm or reject the hypothesis – there may be no reason to collect primary data. Secondary data is usually cheaper and faster to collect, but researchers must always consider its relevance, accuracy, credibility and timeliness.

Primary data is data that is observed or collected directly from first-hand experience. The data must not have been collected previously. The big advantage of primary data is that it relates specifically to the problem at hand. The main disadvantages of primary data are the cost and time required to collect it. Primary data will normally be collected during the next phase of the research process – the formal investigation.

As emphasised above, secondary data should be sought and researched during the preliminary investigation, and all efforts should be made to solve the problem at this stage.

Secondary data can come from internal or external sources. The major internal source is company records. Public libraries, trade associations and government publications are important external sources. Population data, for example, may be obtained from detailed census publications. The Bureau of Market Research at Unisa could, for example, be approached on data such as the average annual household income by population group, annual population increases and growth rates of the South African population, and educational levels by population group.

Primary data can also come from internal or external sources. The major internal source is company personnel. Retailers, wholesalers, customers and competitors are important external sources.

Secondary data collected must clearly relate to the hypotheses formulated earlier.

Example of internal and external sources of information[11]

Examples of internal sources of information are a firm's own records (sales figures, accountancy records, etc.) research reports, in-house experts and experienced sales staff. External sources include trade associations such as the SA Chamber of Business, government departments such as the Department of Trade and Industries and Statistics SA, advertising agencies, consultants, syndicate reports, etc.

Source: Lamb, CJ, Hair, JF, McDaniel, C & Terblanche, N. 2008. *Marketing*. Oxford University Press: South Africa, p 32.

Secondary data on the internet

In the last few years, the rapid development of the Internet has promised the elimination of much of the drudgery associated with the collection of secondary data.

The Internet allows computers (and the people who use them) to access data, pictures, sound and files throughout the world without regard to their physical location or the type of computer on which the data can be found. The World Wide Web (also called the web or www) is one component of the Internet which was designed to make transmission of text and images as easy as possible.

If you know the address of a particular website that contains the secondary data that you are searching for, you can easily access that address by following the correct procedure. Sometimes, however, it can require some hard work and trial and error to find data on the web. However, as long as you have an Internet connection, you have access to a multitude of sources of information.

If the secondary information obtained can provide enough clarification about the hypothesis, it can be accepted or rejected during the preliminary investigation. The problem may therefore be solved at this stage and it may be resolved not to proceed to a formal marketing investigation. However, if it is felt that the problem has not been solved, or if further information is clearly required, the formal investigation must be conducted. In the following example, the data required and possible sources of data are indicated to test certain hypotheses.

A very useful web site that provides a basic introduction to the Internet and search engines is www.learnthenet.co.za

Advantages and limitations of using the Internet for marketing research [12]

Advantages

* A large range of information is provided.
* Information can be accessed rapidly.
* Information can be obtained easily.
* Research costs can be reduced.

➲

Limitations

- The accuracy of the information can be questionable.
- The author of a particular article may be anonymous.
- Useful information can possibly be missed if wrong key words are used.
- Information overload may occur.
- It can be time consuming.
- Organisations may be sensitive about providing information over the Internet.

Source: Adapted from Cant, MC (Ed). 2005. *Marketing research*, 2nd ed. South Africa: New Africa Education, p 78.

Step 5: Select the method of collecting the information

The researcher can gather primary data through observation, experimentation, focus groups and surveys. These methods will be discussed in more detail.

- *Observation method.* The observation method involves recording the behavioural patterns of people, objects and events in a systematic manner to obtain information about the phenomenon of interest. The observer does not question or communicate with the people being observed. Information may be recorded as the events occur or from records of past events. The disadvantages of this method are the cost of waiting for the phenomenon to occur and the difficulty of measuring the phenomenon in a natural setting. For example, a manufacturer of breakfast cereals who wants to study the attention-producing value of new packaging might station observers with cameras and recorders in the supermarket aisles where the cereal is displayed. The observers would monitor the actions of shoppers directly.

Other examples of observational research are as follows:

Observational research[13]

A museum director wanted to know which of the many exhibits was most popular. A survey did not help. Visitors seemed to want to please the interviewer, and usually said that all the exhibits were interesting. Putting observers near exhibits to record how long visitors spent at each one did not help either, since the curious visitors stood around to see what was being recorded, therefore distorting the value of the exercise. Finally, the

↪

museum floors were waxed to a glossy shine. Several weeks later, the floors around the exhibits were inspected. It was easy to tell which exhibits were most popular, based on how much shine had worn off the floor.

A shopping centre developer wondered if one of his shopping centres was attracting customers from all surrounding areas. He hired a company to record the registration numbers of cars in the parking lot. By using this information, the addresses of all shoppers were then obtained and plotted on a map. Very few customers from one particular area were visiting the centre. The developer then aimed direct mail advertising at that area and generated a great deal of new business.

Observation may be more objective than surveys because no questions are asked. The observation method focuses on what people do (direct observation) or on what they did (indirect observation), not on what they say they do or did. Observers, however, can interpret only the behaviour they witness directly, and this interpretation may be inaccurate or biased. A shopper may pick up a package of cereal, examine it and walk away without buying it. The shopper may have wanted to purchase the cereal but may not have had enough money to buy it. An observer, however, might interpret this behaviour as lack of interest in the product. In other words, we do not know why the shopper left the package. Some things such as motives simply cannot be observed.

Artificial observation is often used and is done by way of mechanical or electronic equipment such as the use of the AMPS Peoplemeter II to monitor viewing patterns of selected households in South Africa.[14]

- *Experimentation.* Experimentation research involves testing something in controlled conditions. Conclusions are then drawn about the wider environment. This involves the gathering of primary data by manipulating an independent variable (such as advertising or price) to observe the effect of the change on a dependent variable (such as sales).[15] By attempting to hold all other factors constant while manipulating price, it might be possible to estimate how many units of a product would be demanded at various prices. Researchers often conduct experimentation in a field setting, which is realistic but is difficult to control, and it is almost impossible to ensure that test conditions will be the same as those in the real market.

Experimentation in a field setting

An advertising manager wants to test the effectiveness of a proposed newspaper advertisement, and selects two cities similar in population characteristics, income distribution and so on. One is the control city and the other the test city. The advertisement appears in the test city's newspaper but not in that of the control city. After the advertisement appears, sales of the product are recorded, with any difference in sales being attributed to the advertisement.

Three assumptions in the above situation are made. Firstly, it is possible to find two or more similar cities. Secondly, the control city's environment can be controlled. Thirdly, test conditions are the same as those that will exist when the advertisement is run in the real market. However, locating two almost identical cities for testing is not always easy. Also, if a rival withdraws its product in the control city, sales of the researcher's product might increase. If test city sales are lower than those in the control city, the researcher might incorrectly conclude that the advertisement is ineffective. Thus it is almost impossible to ensure that test conditions will be the same as conditions in the real market.

Let us also look at how experimental research helped to solve the following problem:[16]

Mars chocolate bars: A sweet success

Mars chocolate bar company was losing customers to other sweets and snacks companies, and wanted to identify the reason. Surveys showed that many customers thought that the Mars bar, which was not being sold in a larger size, was too small. They also did not want to pay more for a larger bar. Mars' marketing manager wanted to know if making their chocolate bar bigger would increase sales to offset the higher cost. To decide, they needed more information.

The company carefully varied the size of Mars bars sold in different markets. Otherwise, the marketing mix stayed the same. Researchers then tracked sales in each market to determine the effect of the different sizes. They saw a significant difference immediately. It was clear that the added sales would more than offset the cost of a bigger Mars bar. Marketing managers at Mars therefore made a decision that took them in the opposite direction (of bigger chocolate bars) to other sweets companies.

- *Focus group.* A focus group is the simultaneous involvement of a small number of research participants (usually eight to ten) who interact at the direction of a moderator in order to generate data on a particular issue or topic. This is widely used in exploratory studies. The goal of a focus group is to draw out ideas, feelings and experiences about a certain issue that would be obscured or stifled by more structured methods of data collection. The use of a small group allows the operation of group dynamics, and aids in making the participants feel comfortable in a strange environment.

Focus groups have been useful in understanding basic shifts in consumer lifestyles, values and purchase patterns. Usually the focus group members share homogeneous characteristics such as similarities in age (they may all be in their early 30s), job situations (they may all be sales managers), family composition (they may all have preschool children) or even leisure pursuits (they may all play tennis).

By conducting a group that is as homogeneous as possible with respect to demographic and other characteristics, the researcher is assured that differences in these variables will be less likely to confuse the issue being discussed. The focus group can furnish qualitative data on such things as consumer language, emotional and behavioural reaction to advertising; lifestyle; relationships; the product category and specific brand; and unconscious consumer motivations relative to product design, packaging, promotion or any other facet of the marketing programme being studied. It must, however, be remembered that focus group results are qualitative and not perfectly representative of the general population, thus limiting the reliability of this type of data collection.

Examples of questions in focus group discussions[17]

The following are examples of questions that may be asked during a focus group discussion. Assume the discussion was about department stores.
- What kinds of department stores are there?
- What department stores are you familiar with?
- Which department store is best, worst and why?
- When shopping for a gift in a department store, what is important?
- What is a high-quality product in your terms?
- How much time do you spend in a department store on average per month?

Source: Adapted from Cant, MC (Ed). 2005. *Marketing research*, 2nd ed. South Africa: New Africa Education, p 122.

Cyber focus groups

The newest development in group interviews is the online or cyber focus group. A number of organisations are currently offering this new means of conducting focus groups on the Internet.

Research firms build a database of respondents via a screening question-naire on their website. When a client approaches them with a need for a particular focus group, they access their database and identify individuals who appear to qualify. E-mail is sent to these individuals, asking them to log on to a particular site at a particular time scheduled for the group. A moderator runs the group by typing in questions online for all to see. The group operates in a chat-room type of environment so that all participants see all questions and responses. The complete text of the focus group is captured and is available for review after the group session.

- *Survey method.* Survey research is the gathering of primary data from respondents by mail, by telephone or in person. Survey research can be highly structured or unstructured. In a structured survey, all respondents are asked the same list of questions in the same way. In an unstructured survey, interviewers are free to ask their own questions to encourage respondents to reply as they wish. Three types of data are usually sought in survey research: *facts, opinions* and *motives.* These types of data are explained in the box below.

Types of data in survey research

In a *factual* survey, respondents are asked questions such as: 'What type of car do you drive?'.

In an *opinion* survey, respondents are asked to give opinions, although they believe they are reporting facts. An example of an opinion survey question is: 'What type of toothpaste tastes better?'.

In a *motivational* survey, respondents are asked to interpret and report their motives. These surveys ask 'why' questions such as: 'Why do you holiday in Cape Town every year?'.

Step 6: Design the form for collecting the information

The next step is to design a form or instrument whereby the information is collected. *Mechanical and electronic devices* and *questionnaires* are two types of research instruments used for the collection of primary data:

- *Mechanical and electronic equipment.* Mechanical and electronic equipment are instruments such as galvanometers, tachistoscopes, cameras, and electronic and mechanical meters. These instruments range from simple counting meters (e.g. the number of people passing through a turnstile) to sophisticated reaction-measurement instruments (e.g. emotional reaction to a specific advertisement). Some researchers use personal computers to conduct interviews. Many researchers believe that respondents will provide more private information to a computer than they will in a face-to-face interview.

- *Questionnaires.* These are the most common method for gathering primary data. In designing a questionnaire, researchers must exercise great care in deciding which questions to ask, their content and phrasing, the wording, and how to sequence and format them.

The first important aspect of the questionnaire is *question content and phrasing.* It is important to keep the wording of the questions simple, clear and concise to fit in with the vocabulary level of the respondents.

In surveys conducted among the South African population, for example, the questions should be worded in such a way that even the less sophisticated and less educated understand them. Therefore, it is important to have a clear idea of the target population.

In designing the *wording* of a question, leading questions which may suggest or imply certain answers should be avoided as this could be construed as a cue in the question as to what the answer should be. Often the question can reflect the researcher's viewpoint. A biasing question includes words or phrases that are emotionally coloured and that suggest approval or disapproval, for example: 'Do you agree or disagree with the South African Dental Association's position that advertising presweetened cereal to children is harmful?'. The mere suggestion that an attitude is associated with a prestigious organisation such as the SADA can seriously bias the respondent's reply.

Another important aspect is the *sequence of questions.*[18] This can influence the nature of the respondents' answers and can cause serious errors in the survey findings. It is advisable to use the funnel approach by moving from the general to the particular, since a change of subject may disturb the logical flow of the interview unless there are links between subjects.

The first questions should therefore be simple and should attempt to generate interest, their main intention being to put the respondents at ease and motivate them to react to the succeeding questions without suspicion, Sensitive questions (e.g. income, qualifications and age of the respondent) should be positioned as near to the end of the questionnaire as possible.

The *question format* – that is, the form in which the questions are presented – is also very important. *Open-ended questions* such as those in table 3.1, question form (a), do not provide respondents with a choice of answers; instead respondents formulate their own answers in their own words. *Closed questions* (see table 3.1, question form (b)) give respondents all the possible answers to each question, and they then simply choose one. Ambiguous and leading questions should be avoided, while personal questions, for example the respondent's age, should be placed at the end of the questionnaire (see table 3.1, question form (c)).

Table 3.1 shows a hypothetical questionnaire with commentary about the quality of the questions.[19]

Table 3.1 Examples of open-ended questions, closed questions and faulty questions

Question form (a)	Question form (b)	Question form (c)
1. **Totally open** What do you think of Toyota South Africa? _____ _____	1. **Dichotomous** Do you think air bags should be required equipment in all new cars? Yes ☐ No ☐	1. **What is your age?** This is too personal a question to begin a questionnaire. It should be at the end and provide age ranges.
2. **Sentence completion** In buying a second-hand car, the most important thing to keep in mind is _____	2. **Multiple choice** What age group are you in? 20 or under ☐ 21 to 29 ☐ 30 to 39 ☐ 40 to 49 ☐ 50 to 59 ☐ 60 or over ☐	2. **What kind of car(s) do you presently own?** This is an ambiguous question. What does 'kind' mean? Brand name, size, model, country of origin, convertible or hard top? What if the respondent leases instead of owns?
3. **Word association** Domestic cars _____ Foreign cars _____ Auto dealerships _____ Ford _____	3. **Semantic differential** Ford of South Africa Large … Small … Modern … Old-fashioned …	3. **How much did you pay for security equipment the last time you bought a new car?** The respondent will probably be unable to provide this information.
4. **Picture completion**	4. **Rating scale** Customer service at Ford dealers is: 1 … Excellent 2 … Very good 3 … Good 4 … Fair 5 … Poor	4. **Don't you think passive restraint systems make for safer and more economical cars than other types of systems?** Yes ☐ No ☐ What does 'passive restraint' mean? Two subjects are mentioned here – safety and economy. It is also a leading question.
		5. **Have you ever felt guilty for driving your car after you had too much to drink, thereby inviting a serious accident?** Yes ☐ No ☐ Most people would probably not be willing to answer this question.

Source: Adapted from Schoell, WIF & Guiltinan, JP in Cant, MC (Ed). 2004. *Essentials of marketing*, 2nd ed. Cape Town: Juta, p 103.

Validity and reliability should always be considered in questionnaire development. *Validity* refers to the degree to which a study accurately reflects or assesses the specific concept that the researcher is attempting to measure. *Reliability* is concerned with the accuracy of the actual measuring instrument or procedure.

Pretesting of the questionnaire is essential if the researcher is to be satisfied that the questionnaire designed will perform its various functions. The questionnaire is tested on a small sample of respondents to identify and eliminate potential problems – this helps to reveal errors while they can still be easily corrected. It should be tried out on a selected group similar in composition to the one that will ultimately be sampled.

There are various *contact methods*. When the questionnaire has been designed, a decision must be made on how to contact the survey participants. Survey research data can be obtained from mail, via e-mail, telephone or personal interview. Table 3.2 shows the relative advantages and disadvantages of various surveys, some of which are now discussed.

- *Mail survey.* This is a relatively low-cost self-administered study both delivered and returned via mail. For mail surveys, a questionnaire is mailed to possible respondents, and the completed questionnaire is returned by mail to the researcher. Mail surveys are flexible in their application and relatively low in cost, but the major disadvantage is the problem of non-response error. When the geographical area to be covered is large, time is not a major factor, and the questionnaire is relatively short, a mail survey is favoured. Respondents can answer at their convenience, and there are no personal interviews to bias the results. Mail and fax questionnaires are particularly versatile in reaching all types of people in remote geographical areas. E-mail is another form of mail survey that is gaining ground; however, its use is, of course, limited to those respondents who have e-mail.
- *Telephone survey.* In a telephone survey, an interviewer asks the respondents questions over the telephone. This type of interview is efficient and economical, and, compared to the personal interview, reduces the potential for bias. The basic limitation of the telephone interview relates to the limited amount of data that can be obtained. Technological advances are making telephone surveys less costly and time consuming; many research firms are working with data entry terminals, The interviewers read the questions off the video screen and enter the respondents' answers on the computer.
- *Personal survey.* In a personal survey the interviewer asks questions of the respondents in a face-to-face situation. The interviewer's task is to contact the respondent, ask the questions and record the responses. Face-to-face interviews may cause respondents to bias their responses because of a desire to please or impress the interviewer. It is also an expensive method involving extensive planning and control. However, the personal interview method renders the best response in most cases.

- *Internet survey.* In an Internet survey, respondents are recruited over the Internet from potential respondent databases developed by the research firm or via conventional means. Specific target individuals may be contacted by telephone or mail and asked to access a particular web location to complete the survey. This survey has certain similarities to a mail survey in terms of its basic advantages and disadvantages. However, in the cyber survey there is the potential for interactivity and the ability to expose respondents to various stimuli (e.g. print advertisements, audio for radio advertisements, product and packaging designs and so on). Cyber surveys have the following advantages: speed, cost effectiveness, broad geographic scope, accessibility and tracking. However, there may be sample control problems with Internet surveys.

Table 3.2 Characteristics of various types of survey research[20]

Characteristic	Personal surveys	Mall intercepts	Telephone surveys	Mail surveys	Focus groups
Cost	High	High	Moderate to low	Moderate	Low
Time span	Moderate	Moderate	Fast	Slow	Fast
Use of interviewer probes	Yes	Yes	Yes	No	Yes
Ability to show concepts to respondent	Yes	Yes	No	Limited	Yes
Management control over interviewer	Low	Moderate	Low	N/a	High
General data quality	High	Moderate	Moderate to low	Moderate	Moderate
Ability to collect large amounts of data	Low	Moderate	Moderate to low	High	Moderate
Ability to handle complex questions	High	Moderate	Moderate	Low	Low

Source: Lamb, CJ et al. 2008. *Marketing.* South Africa: Oxford University Press, p 111.

Step 7: Determine the extent of the formal investigation

In this step, the extent of the formal investigation must be determined. This focuses on the design of the *sampling plan.* Sampling involves selecting representative units from a total population. Marketers can predict the reactions of a total market or market segment by systematically focusing on a limited number of units. This is called *sampling.* However, we must first clarify some of the terms which are relevant to sampling.

The group that the marketer is interested in knowing something about is referred to as the *population* or *universe.* Sometimes a population is small enough that marketers or researchers may study all of the members of the population in order to learn whatever it is they are interested in establishing. In such cases, the whole population or universe can be investigated.

When the population or universe is extremely large, it may be more convenient to study a subset of the population, called a *sample*. A sample is therefore a set of items, called *units,* selected from the population.

Example of a census

A study on the marketing knowledge of supermarket retailers who are members of Nafcoc revealed that only 200 Nafcoc members were supermarket retailers. Since this population was relatively small, all of the members were studied, so this was a census.

Examples of a sample

If the expenditure of households in Soweto is being researched, the researcher may include all the households in Soweto, in which case a census is taken (the sum total of all households in Soweto). However, the researcher may also decide to interview only some of these households, for example 10% of the households, which is termed a sample.

A shoe manufacturer who wanted to study the brand preferences of all teenagers between 13 and 16 years of age found it almost impossible to research all of them and decided to draw a sample of 2 500 teenagers.

When researchers establish a sample, it is crucial to select respondents who will represent the population of interest. This is known as a *sample frame.*

The *sample size* refers to how many respondents should be incorporated in the study, and is an important consideration for researchers. No fixed rules exist concerning the number of units to be included. However, there are general norms and guidelines in this regard. Samples which are applied in consumer research can often be less than 1% of the population, on condition that a probability sample and statistical formulae are used. In the case of industrial research, however, larger samples are used because the number of industrial clients is considerably smaller than in the case of final consumers.

In this step of the research process, a decision is needed about the type of sample. A good sampling plan will produce a sample that is representative of the characteristics of the population from which it is drawn. Two basic types of samples are probability (random) samples and non-probability (non-random) samples.

A *probability* (or *random*) sample is a selection in which each item in a population has a known chance of being included through strict statistical procedures. It is the best way to ensure a representative sample. The following random sampling methods can be employed: simple random sampling, stratified random sampling and cluster sampling. *Simple random sampling* involves a probability sample in which each element has a known and equal chance of selection.

A simple random sample

To draw a simple random sample of ten flats from a block of flats, the researcher should incorporate the flat numbers into a list of the total population (all flats). Flat numbers will then be drawn at random until the prescribed sample size has been reached

In the case of *stratified random sampling,* the population is divided into mutually exclusive subgroups (strata) on the basis of common characteristics. The basis used for stratification (e.g. age, income, occupation and gender) must be a characteristic relevant to the research project.

Example of random sampling error[21]

Assume that a research population consists of 100 elements or people of which 50% are male and 50% are female. If a sample of ten elements was drawn using the simple random sampling method, it is possible that it would consist of three males and seven females. Even though all the sampling procedures were followed exactly, the sample does not represent the population. As the sample size increases, the sample will become more representative of the population.

Source: Adapted from Cant, MC (Ed). 2005. *Marketing research*, 2nd ed, South Africa: New Africa Education, p 90.

In *cluster sampling*, the procedure is different. Simple random sampling treats each population element individually, while stratified sampling treats elements in groups of the population individually. In the case of cluster sampling, the population will be grouped into clusters, and only some of the groups will be randomly selected for study,

The grouping of clusters is done according to ease or availability, and should be heterogeneous (different) within subgroups and externally homogeneous (similar).

Stratified random sampling

Suppose you were studying leisure activities of people in the population and you believed that age was relevant. You would stratify the population by age. People in a particular stratum would be of similar ages, and each stratum would differ from the others with respect to age. You could then use simple random sampling to select sampling units from each stratum. Clearly you would need more information on the population to select a stratified sample than to select a simple sample.

A *non-probability* (or *non-random*) sample is a selection in which not every item in a population has a known chance of being included because researcher judgement enters into the selection. The sample's representativeness depends on how good the researcher's judgement is. Non-probability sampling can take two forms: *convenience sampling* and *judgement sampling*. In the case of convenience sampling, the sampling units are chosen simply on the basis of convenience, for example:

Example of convenience sampling

Convenience sampling is used in the case of on-the-street interviews, for example asking people in a supermarket their opinions about a new brand of detergent, or conducting taste tests on cheese. People who are not at the same place as the interviewer, and people who are not in that particular supermarket at the time when opinions or taste reactions are being sought, do not have a chance of being included in the sample.

In the case of *judgement sampling*, units are chosen on the basis of the researcher's opinion as to their representativeness.

Judgement sampling

Examples of judgement sampling include selecting a sample of salespeople for their opinions as input to preparing a sales forecast, and selecting cities in which to test market new products. The representativeness of these samples depends on the researcher's judgement in selecting the sampling units.

Step 8: Select, train and control the interviewers

In this step of the marketing research process, the research design is implemented – that is, the data is collected. Data collection is often the most expensive aspect of the research process, and the possibility of error is high. Interviewers thus have to be carefully selected and trained, and an important control task has to be performed.

In the *selection* of interviewers it is advisable to establish specific selection criteria. These will depend on the nature of the questionnaire, the type of respondent who is interviewed and factors relating specifically to the investigation. For example, for open-ended questions which require probing, experienced interviewers are required.

Interviewers need *training* to ensure that they all administer the questionnaire in the same manner so that the data can be collected uniformly. The training should cover making the initial contact, asking the questions, probing, recording the answers and terminating the interview.

Control of the interviewers should be exercised continuously. The potential for error in data collection is very high. To help ensure that the research design is being implemented correctly, the researcher must monitor and control every phase of its implementation. In a personal interview survey, for example, it is important to monitor the fieldwork. The researcher might take a sample of completed questionnaires and call the respondents to verify that they were, in fact, interviewed.

Training interviewers

In a research investigation into the marketing knowledge of supermarket retailers, the interviewers were given instructions as follows:

1. Speak to the store owner/manager/person in charge of the store upon entering the store.
2. Identify yourself.
3. Explain what you are doing.
4. Hand the respondent the letter of introduction, or read it aloud if necessary.
5. Complete the front page (name of store, owner, and so on).
6. Ask all the questions.
7. Record responses by following the instruction below each question – for example tick more than one item if necessary.
8. Do not influence the respondent when asking the questions.

Step 9: Fieldwork

The information is now actually being collected from the respondents. Various problems may occur during the interviewing process, such as non-response error, respondent bias and interviewer bias, which are now discussed in more detail.

- *Non-response error.* A great percentage of respondents may not act in response to the research. Non-response errors occur when the results of the respondents who participated in the research contrast from what the results would have been if all the respondents who were initially selected in the sample participated in the research.
- *Respondent bias.* Interviewers should do their best to obtain answers that are honest and as accurate as possible. Some respondents may be inclined to pre-empt the interviewer by providing answers that they think the interviewer is looking for. This bias should be addressed when the interviewer is trained.
- *Interviewer bias.* Interviewer bias can take many forms, for example their tone of voice, age, gender or way of interviewing may unconsciously result in bias. Conscious interviewer bias can also occur. For example, the interviewers may

complete the questionnaires themselves. This type of interviewer bias can be limited by thorough training, selecting highly motivated interviewers and exercising strict control during the fieldwork.

Step 10: Data processing

When the fieldwork has been completed, the data must be processed. Data processing entails editing and coding the collected data to facilitate analysis. Editors go through completed questionnaires to eliminate those answered by the wrong respondents and to check for readability of the responses. Editing also involves setting up categories for the data in accordance with the research design. Coding assigns the data to proper categories as explained in the box below:

Categories for data

For example, in a survey of cigarette smokers to determine brand usage, the categories might consist of brands, types of cigarettes (filtered, unfiltered, menthol), city size, household income and gender of respondent.
Proper categories for the brands may include:

- Stuyvesant 20s might be coded brand number 1.
- Satin Leaf Lights 30s might be coded brand number 2.

Proper categories for the cities may include:

- Cities consisting of 20 000 people or less might be coded city size number 1.
- Cities with one million or more people, number 2, and so on.

Sometimes questionnaires are pre-coded by printing the codes on the questionnaires to assist data entry terminal personnel in entering responses directly from the questionnaire. Data-processing activities are usually done by means of computers. Thus the data is often put into a computer-readable form and then read into a computer file and stored.

Data analysis is done next. This is the process of editing and reducing accumulated data to a manageable size, developing summaries, looking for patterns and applying statistical techniques. Data-analysis techniques should be planned in advance of data collection as part of the research design. For example, more data might be collected if computers are used than if the analysis is done manually.

More sophisticated data-analysis techniques may also be used as the researcher moves beyond the description of the data to complex statistical analysis of them. Cross-tabulations are often used to show how one variable relates to another. For example, two-way tabulations provide answers to such questions as: 'What is the relationship between gender and brand loyalty in the motor vehicle market?'.

> **Statistics on the Internet**
>
> There is a tremendous amount of statistical information and advice available over the Internet. The web is becoming a very useful source of information for the selection of appropriate statistical techniques for a particular problem, the proper use of different statistical techniques and emerging statistical techniques, In addition, news and special-interest groups can be an excellent source of information and advice regarding the proper use of statistical procedures.

Step 11: Communicate information to the decision maker

The final step in the research process involves interpreting the findings and communicating this information to the marketing manager. Communication problems between researchers and marketing managers often arise due to their different backgrounds and work environments. Inevitably, the written research report is the document that management will use as its information source in making a decision.

> **Publishing research reports on the Internet**
>
> Some companies and research companies publish marketing research reports on the Internet. This has become extremely easy because all the latest versions of the major word-processing, presentation graphics and spreadsheet packages (e.g. Microsoft Office and Lotus SmartSuite) are easy to use.
>
> Publishing reports on the Internet provides qualified users worldwide instant access to these documents. Users can view the marketing research reports on screen and also have full access to supporting audio, video and animation features. They can save the reports for future reference or for more careful analysis at a later stage. Complete reports or portions of reports can be printed out in hard copy if desired.

3.5 Market potential and sales forecasting

In this last section of the chapter, we deal with a specific element of marketing information, namely market potential and sales forecasting. This is a specialised field, and therefore we will look at only some basic concepts and procedures.[22]

When an enterprise observes a new market trend based on the information obtained from marketing research or the marketing information system, it is essential that the current size and future potential of the new market demand be determined. Knowledge of market sizes and probable growth patterns provide the basis for the selection of attractive markets and would thus help in the formulation of appropriate marketing strategies for those markets.

The extent to which plans can be successfully implemented depends not only on managers' abilities in setting and implementing strategies but more fundamentally on their ability to predict the market accurately. This means two things: firstly, assessing the market potential – that is, working out how big the total market is – and, secondly, forecasting sales – that is, calculating how big a slice of that market the organisation can obtain.

Market potential focuses on the current size and characteristics of the market, whereas *sales forecasting* looks at the future market situation.

3.5.1 Levels of market measurement

The size of a market (in other words, the potential or demand) can be measured on different levels, and it is important to clearly state beforehand what type of market is involved. Market measurement can be determined by consumer level, product level, geographic level and time level. Marketing managers must clearly define the required level of measurement as this would impact directly on the formulation of resulting marketing decision making. Consider the following example of the possible levels of market measurement for Coca-Cola.

Possible levels of market measurement for Coca-Cola

- *Consumer level.* The consumer level of demand measurement is the most popular level used as it provides information on the number of final consumers defined in different market segments. Coca-Cola would, for example, be interested in the demand for Coke in schools, at sports meetings and among fitness fanatics.
- *Product level.* On the product level, an enterprise can measure consumer demand for one brand or for all of its brands in a given product category. As most markets are targeted by various formats of the same product, the demand measurement can be expressed in terms of the total number of current buyers for each product type. Coca-Cola, for example, would be interested in the sales of all soft drinks in the RSA – sales of Coca-Cola, sales of Coke Light, sales of Tab and so on.
- *Geographic level.* On the geographic level, the total market can be divided into geographical segments and it is thus possible to express the demand measurement in geographic terms. Coca-Cola may be interested in certain areas such as the Cape metropolitan area, Kwa-Zulu-Natal, the RSA and southern Africa.
- *Time level.* A demand measurement should also be specific in terms of the time of purchase, and should provide information on the sales over different time periods. Coca-Cola may be interested in monthly sales, seasonal sales and annual sales.

3.5.2 Relevant markets for measurement

The different types of markets which can be measured are not all relevant to a specific enterprise. It depends on whether the enterprise is actively involved or interested in the particular market. It is thus necessary to distinguish the relevant markets that can be used in estimating market potential:

- *Total market* (also referred to as the *market potential*) pertains to all actual and potential buyers of a product type if it is generally available and offered for purchase, and whether consumers have the ability to buy. For example, the total market for Coke is the RSA in total.
- *Available market* refers only to those actual and potential buyers of a product who have the interest, income and ability to buy the product at a particular point in time (e.g. metropolitan areas where consumers are able to buy the product because of its availability and their level of income).
- *Target market* is that part of the available market to which the company has chosen to direct its marketing activities (e.g. the 16- to 35-year-old age group). The target market for Coke may include only those parts of the metropolitan population that fall into particular age groups and lifestyle categories.
- *Penetrated market* refers to the number of consumers who have already bought the product. Coke's penetrated market refers to that section of the target market that has already bought the product.

3.5.3 Market and sales potential

We first need to clarify the concepts 'market potential' and 'sales potential' before we look at ways of estimating or measuring market and sales potential.

- *Market potential.* This is concerned with what is possible; in other words, it focuses on the current size of the market. Market potential is *the maximum possible sales of a specific product in a specific market over a specific period for all sellers in the industry.*

  It assumes that all sellers are presenting their maximum marketing effort under a given set of environmental conditions. Market potential thus sets an upper limit for industry sales. This definition of market potential raises problems in calculating a figure for market potential, as it involves many assumptions about competitors and the environment and because it needs a precise definition of 'the market'. In addition, methods of quantifying the variables concerned are also required.

  Market potential data helps in evaluating which opportunities the marketer should pursue, for example in determining which market segments to target. Such data also helps in deciding the level of marketing effort that should be committed to the various segments and in providing benchmarks for evaluating performance in selected segments.

Market potential for beer

Market potential in the beer industry can refer to one or more of the following markets:

- Total sales of beer.
- Total sales of a particular form of beer (light, dark).
- An entire market.
- Only a segment of that market.

A segment, in turn, can be defined in terms of any of the segmentation variables, for example the market potential in city A only could be estimated. Alternatively, we could estimate market potential within a certain age or income segment of people in city A.

The toy industry reviewing its definition of the market[23]

In the early 1990s, the traditional toy industry was reviewing its definition of the market following a report that children were leaving the traditional toy market earlier and earlier, and that their needs, wants and consumption choices were broadening. This means that toy manufacturers are competing directly with clothing, trainers, videos, electronic games, and so on, for children's disposable income. The toy manufacturers now have to consider themselves in the youth gift market, not just the toy market.

- *Sales potential.* Even after the potential has been estimated for the market as a whole (market potential), a company will then need to determine its own *sales potential* – that is, the share of the market that it could reasonably capture. Sales potential is *the upper limit of sales that a firm could possibly reach for a specific product in a specific market over a specific time period.* It is based on a maximum level of marketing effort and an assumed set of environmental conditions. A company's sales potential, therefore, is the share of market potential that it might capture if it maximised its marketing effort. Sales potential is therefore partly a result of the company's marketing effort and its success in attracting and holding customers.

Having a clear idea of market and sales potential provides a useful input to the marketing planning process. It is especially important for planning selling efforts and allocating resources. The allocation of sales force effort and the establishment of distribution point and service support centres, for example, can reflect sales potential rather than actual sales, thus allowing scope for expansion. Similarly, sales potential can also be used to plan sales territories, quotas, sales force compensation and targets for prospecting.

3.5.4 Estimating market and sales potential

The methods used for estimating market and sales potential depend on how new or innovative the product or service is, and how mature the market is. We distinguish between the breakdown methods and build-up methods.

- *Breakdown methods.* The most common breakdown method used to estimate market and sales potential is *total market measurement.* This begins with any total industry or market data that may be available from secondary research. This information is then broken down to market segment level and thereafter to the company's own sales potential. This method relies heavily on the availability of a long series of data on industry sales volume and consumption by segments within that market, but rarely is such complete and detailed data available. Potential is thus often estimated from what data is available and then adjusted to take account of the current marketing environment. Once market and segment potentials have been established, sales potential can be derived by estimating competitors' relative market share and then calculating how this might change as a result of expected actions, for example a new product launch.
- *Build-up methods.* There are three main methods for estimating reliable market and sales potential figures: census, survey and secondary data:
  - The *census method* is based on a detailed consideration of every buyer and potential buyer in a market. This may be difficult in mass consumer markets, but is more feasible in industrial situations. The market potential is effectively the sum of all the potentials estimated for individual purchasers.
  - The *survey method* is more widely used in consumer markets where a representative sample of consumers is asked about purchase intentions. This information can then be used as a basis for calculating total market or sales potential. The main problem, however, is that respondents might not be truthful about their intentions.
  - *Secondary data* can be used to establish sales and market potential. Internal sales records can be used to predict individual customers' purchasing on the basis of past behaviour. In this approach, the sales potentials are produced first and the market potential is then derived from those figures.

3.5.5 Market and sales forecasting

The terms *market forecast* and *sales forecast* must be defined before we consider the development of a sales forecast.

- *Market forecast.* A market forecast is *an estimate of the expected sales of a specific product in a specific market over a specific time period for all sellers in the industry.* It is based on an expected level of industry effort and an expected set of environmental conditions. In other words, the market forecast is the portion of market potential that is expected to be realised.
- *Sales forecast.* A sales forecast is *an estimate of the number of units a firm expects to reach for a specific product in a specific market over a specific time period.* It is based on an intended level and type of marketing effort by the company and an expected set of environmental conditions.

Marketing often plays a central role in preparing and disseminating forecasts. This is perhaps one of its most important functions, as the sales and market forecasts provided are the basis of all subsequent planning and decision making within most areas of the company.

Examples of forecasts

- A car manufacturer wanting to forecast the demand for each model in the product line.
- A tour operator wanting to forecast the demand for specific destinations.
- A university wanting to forecast numbers of full-time, part-time and overseas students by programme offered by the university.

The forecast is the starting point for all subsequent decisions. If this is not done correctly, the whole company can encounter major capacity or cash-flow problems.

Some problematic forecasting situations

- In fashion markets it can be very difficult to forecast what styles are going to sell and in what quantities, hence the popularity of 'end of season' sales as retailers try to sell off surplus stock.
- Holiday companies and airlines also find forecasting difficult, and again find themselves selling off surplus holidays or seats on aircraft at discounted rates. This occurs until actual departure dates.

There is no such thing as a rigid or absolute forecast. Different forecasters using different forecasting methods are almost certain to reach different results. Forecasts should, however, share some common characteristics. They should:

- be based upon historical information from which a projection can be made;
- look forward over a specific, clearly defined time period; and
- make clearly specified assumptions, since uncertainty characterises the future.

3.5.6 Forecasting methods

There are several forecasting methods. Rather than relying on only one, planners often use a number of methods. We will briefly consider the sales-force survey, expert survey and time series analysis.

- *Sales-force surveys* can provide a wealth of information. Such surveys involve asking sales representatives to provide forecasts on customers, dealers, accounts and so on. The sales force is a valuable source of expert opinion, since representatives are very close to customers on a daily basis and will learn of likely changes in purchasing intentions early. The main problems of these surveys are bias and naivety.
- *Expert surveys* can be used by bringing outside expertise into the sales-forecasting process. The expert survey is the sales-forecasting method that involves the participation of people outside the firm who have special knowledge and experience in the market under consideration. This includes economists, consultants and retired executives.
- *Time series analysis* is a means of using historical data to predict the future. Analysis of historic data can reveal patterns in the organisation's sales figures. These patterns include trends, cycles, seasonality and random factors. In the case of *trends*, for example, extrapolation of data on a straight- or curved-line basis can give a broad view of the general direction in which sales are moving. *Cycles* reflect periodic changes in patterns over a period of time. *Seasonality* – that is, shorter-term fluctuations around an overall trend – may even be observed on a daily or weekly basis, if that is what the organisation requires. Any forecast must make allowances for *random factors* such as strikes, riots and civil commotion (especially in the insurance industry).

Summary

In this chapter, we focused firstly on the information needs of marketers and how they gather and use that information to develop marketing strategies. More specifically, we dealt with the marketing information system.

We also looked at the factors involved when a company decides to conduct marketing research, and the research techniques available to gather the specific information it needs. The steps in the marketing research process were dealt with comprehensively. We also looked at the important role of the Internet in marketing research. Finally, we examined market potential and sales forecasting, a specific element of marketing information.

References

1. Nieuwenhuizen, C, Rossouw, D & Badenhorst, J. 2008. *Business management: A contemporary approach*. Cape Town: Juta, p 164.

2. McDaniel, C & Gates, R. 2007. *Marketing research essentials*, 6th ed. San Francisco: John Wiley & Sons.
3. Ibid.
4. Brink, A. 1997. *The marketing perception of grocery store retailers belonging to black business associations in Gauteng.* Unpublished thesis for the DCom degree. Pretoria: Unisa, pp 124–126.
5. AMPS. 2009. South African consumer database, *Eighty20.* [Online] Available from: http://www.eighty20.co.za/databases/show_db.cgi?db=amps2008#s (downloaded on 19 February 2009).
6. Cant, MC (Ed). 2004. *Essentials of marketing,* 2nd ed. Cape Town: Juta.
7. Ibid.
8. Cooper, DR & Schindler, PS. 2006. *Business research methods*, 9th ed. New York: McGraw-Hill.
9. Strydom, JW (Ed). 2004. *Introduction to marketing,* 3rd ed. Cape Town: Juta.
10. Schoell, WF & Guiltinan, JP in Cant, MC (Ed). 2004. *Essentials of marketing,* 2nd ed. Cape Town: Juta.
11. Lamb, CJ, Hair, JF, McDaniel, C & Terblanche, N. 2008. *Marketing.* South Africa: Oxford University Press.
12. Cant, MC (Ed). 2005. *Marketing research,* 2nd ed. Claremont: New Africa Education.
13. Strydom, JW (Ed). 2004. *Introduction to marketing,* 3rd ed. Cape Town: Juta.
14. Cant, MC, Strydom, JW, Jooste, CJ & Du Plessis, PJ. 2006. *Marketing management,* 5th ed. Cape Town: Juta.
15. Schoell, WF & Guiltinan, JP in Cant, MC (Ed). 2004. *Essentials of marketing,* 2nd ed. Cape Town: Juta.
16. Strydom, JW (Ed). 2004. *Introduction to marketing,* 3rd ed. Cape Town: Juta.
17. Cant, MC (Ed). 2005. *Marketing research,* 2nd ed. Claremont: New Africa Education.
18. Ibid.
19. Cant, MC (Ed). 2004. *Essentials of marketing,* 2nd ed. Cape Town: Juta.
20. Lamb, CJ et al. 2008. *Marketing.* South Africa: Oxford University Press.
21. Cant, MC (Ed). 2005. *Marketing research,* 2nd ed. Claremont: New Africa Education.
22. Schoell, WF & Guiltinan, JP in Cant, MC (Ed). 2004. *Essentials of marketing,* 2nd ed. Cape Town: Juta.
23. Brassington, F & Pettitt, S. 2006. *Principles of marketing,* 4th ed. Prentice Hall.

Consumer and business behaviour

CHAPTER **FOUR**

Learning outcomes

After you have studied this chapter you will be able to:

- describe the individual factors that influence the behaviour of individual consumers;
- explain which group factors can influence consumer behaviour with regard to cultural, peer, reference and family groups;
- analyse, step-by-step, the decision-making process and indicate what happens after a product or service has been purchased;
- indicate how buyers take decisions in the industrial purchasing process; and
- explain how consumer behaviour differs from business buying behaviour.

4.1 Introduction

The question of what the thought processes are that result in consumers' decision to buy or not to buy has interested marketing management for many years. Prospective buyers are usually exposed to a number of product sales pitches, which they then, in their own unique way, internalise or consider before making a decision to purchase a product or not. This process of internalisation is referred to as a 'black box' because we cannot see into a buyer's mind, which means that marketing management can apply the stimuli (advertising message) and observe the response of the consumer (purchase decision), but cannot witness the consumer's actual decision-making process. The classic model of buyer behaviour is called a stimulus-response model (figure 4.1).

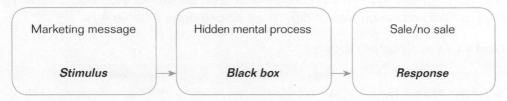

Figure 4.1 Stimulus-response model of consumer behaviour

This model assumes that consumers will respond in some predictable manner to the stimuli. Unfortunately, it does not tell us why they buy or do not buy the product – this information is concealed in the 'black box'.

Marketing management seeks to understand as much as possible about the mental process that yields the consumers' responses, which requires a thorough knowledge and understanding of what determines consumers' needs and how they respond to satisfy them.

The marketer has to have a thorough understanding of consumer behaviour. This field studies how individuals, groups and organisations select, buy, use and dispose of goods, services, ideas or experiences to satisfy their needs and desires. Understanding consumer behaviour is not simple. Customers may state their needs and desires but act otherwise. They may respond to influences that change their decisions at the last minute. Marketers must nevertheless study their target consumers' wants, perceptions, and shopping and buying behaviour.[1]

While the needs, demands and preferences of each individual are unique, there are also many common or similar behaviour patterns, and all consumers follow more or less the same course when decisions must be taken. In decision making, all people are influenced to a greater or lesser extent by the actions of others with whom they come into contact. The unique, inherent qualities of consumers, the phases in the consumer decision-making process and societal influences are discussed in this chapter.

The behaviour patterns of a typical consumer differ from those of the user of industrial products and services. While a consumer often decides to purchase products for emotional reasons, the industrial consumer only buys those products that are really required in further production processes. In this chapter, a distinction is drawn between consumer behaviour and that of industrial buyers (business buying behaviour).

Marketing management needs extensive information on and knowledge of consumer and buyer behaviour in order to focus the market offering specifically on final consumers or, alternatively, on industrial buyers. Marketing management can, in turn, influence society as the need to own desirable products can motivate consumers to try to improve their lifestyle.

4.2 Types of purchase decisions

Consumer decision making varies with the type of purchase decision. Assael[2] distinguished four types of purchase decisions based on the degree of buyer involvement and the degree of difference among brands (table 4.1).

Table 4.1 Types of purchase decisions

	High involvement	Low involvement
Significant differences between brands	Complex purchasing behaviour	Variety-seeking purchasing behaviour
Few differences between brands	Dissonance-reducing behaviour	Habitual purchasing behaviour

Source: Adapted from Assael, H. 1987. *Consumer behaviour and marketing action*. Boston: Kent, p 87.

- *Complex purchasing behaviour.* Consumers engage in complex purchasing behaviour when they are highly involved in a purchase and aware of significant differences among brands. This is usually the case when the product is expensive, being bought infrequently, involves risk and is self-expressive (e.g. cars, computers, clothes, furniture and electronic equipment). Buyers need assistance in learning about the product's attributes and benefits.
- *Dissonance-reducing behaviour.* Buyers are highly involved in the purchase, but believe that there are few differences between the brands. The buyer will shop around to determine what is available on the market but will buy fairly quickly (e.g. lawnmowers and tiles).
- *Habitual purchasing behaviour.* Buyers demonstrate low involvement, and significant brand differences are absent. Buyers buy out of habit but are not brand loyal (e.g. salt, milk, bread and deodorant). The products are mostly low-cost, frequent purchases.
- *Variety-seeking purchasing behaviour.* These buying situations are characterised by low consumer involvement but significant brand differences. Consumers do a great deal of brand switching for the sake of variety (e.g. takeaway food, restaurants, ice cream, entertainment, salad dressing and coffee).[3]

Two further types of decision making also occur:

- *Routine decision making.* This occurs when a consumer, without consciously thinking about it, consistently purchases the same branded products. This loyalty to specific branded products is the result of the extended decision-making process of the preceding period. Routine purchasing reduces the necessity of repeating the decision-making process each time an item is needed, thereby facilitating the purchasing task. Household necessities which must be restocked regularly, such as toiletries, detergents, margarine, coffee and tea, are often purchased on this basis.
- *Impulsive decision making.* This implies unplanned action on the spur of the moment, in contrast to the purposeful planning visible in true decision making, but this is not completely correct. In impulsive decision making, the consumer also progresses through all the phases of the decision-making process. Usually, action follows immediately after the decision has been reached, and to a bystander it seems as though planning (which includes purposefully searching for and evaluating information) did not precede the action. Impulsive action viewed in this light indicates a decision made at the point of purchase and therefore cannot be regarded as an irresponsible approach to purchasing. It can be concluded that decision making is lengthy when the decision is deemed important. Decision making can also occur spontaneously when the consumer impulsively buys immediately after becoming aware of an unsatisfied need.

4.3 Factors influencing consumer behaviour

Several individual and group factors strongly influence the decision-making process. Figure 4.2 summarises these influences.

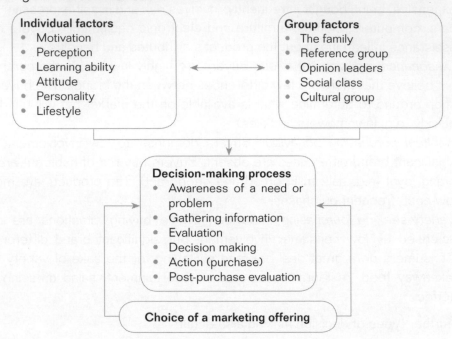

Figure 4.2 Overview of consumer behaviour

Source: Cant et al. 2006. *Marketing management*. Cape Town: Juta, p 74.

4.3.1 *Individual factors influencing consumer buying decisions*

Individual factors refer to factors inherent in human behaviour that will influence an individual's behaviour as a consumer.

4.3.1.1 Motivation

All behaviour starts with needs and wants. *Needs are the basic forces that motivate an individual to do something. Wants are needs that are learned during an individual's lifetime.* Everyone, for example, needs some kind of liquid to quench their thirst. Some people have learned to want mineral water, others a soft drink and others either coffee or tea. A *motive* is a need or want that is sufficiently stimulated to move an individual to seek satisfaction. Hunger that is strong enough to move the consumer to seek out a takeaway meal, and fear of burglary great enough that the consumer seeks security by installing an alarm system, are examples of aroused needs/wants that become motives for behaviour.

It is sometimes quite easy to identify the motives that underlie a buying decision, while at other times it is impossible to identify these motives. Buying motives may be grouped into three different levels, depending on the consumer's awareness of them and their willingness to divulge them:

- *Awareness need level.* Consumers know their motives and are quite willing to talk about them.
- *Pre-awareness need level.* Consumers are aware of the motives but will not reveal them to others.
- *Unawareness need level.* Consumers cannot explain the factors motivating their buying actions because they are unaware of these motives, or they are subconscious motives.

To further complicate the situation, a purchase is often the result of multiple motives, some even in conflict with one another. In buying a new car, the young buyer searches not only for economy and affordability, but also for comfort and luxury.

The best known and also the most accepted theory of classifying the diversity of needs is that of Maslow. He classified human needs in a scheme in which the lower-level needs must first be satisfied, or partly satisfied, before the higher-level needs can fully emerge. Figure 4.3 shows Maslow's hierarchy of needs.

The lowest-level needs are physiological, which help to ensure the survival of the individual. The highest level is reflected in the desire for self-actualisation. According to this theory, the individual is motivated to fulfil whichever need is most strongly felt at any given moment.

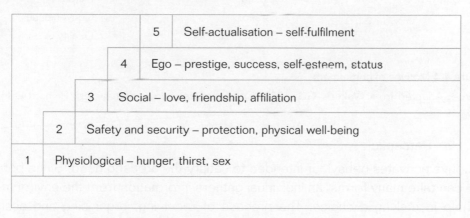

Figure 4.3 Maslow's hierarchy of needs
Source: Adapted from Maslow, AH. 1954. *Motivation and personality.* New York: Harper & Row.

The following motives (human needs) appear in figure 4.3:

- *A basic physiological need,* hunger, compels the consumer to purchase food.
- *Safety needs* motivate the consumer to erect a security fence, take out insurance, and be concerned about his or her health.

- *Social needs* underlie a host of purchasing decisions, from cosmetics to deodorants.
- *Ego needs* cause the consumer to purchase luxury products as symbols of status and success.
- *Self-actualisation* is the highest human need and has to do with personal development and individuality. It is unfortunately true that few people are in a position to satisfy this need. Enrolling for art classes is an example of an attempt to express individuality.

Consumers are not always motivated by psychological needs; they are also concerned about more rational drivers such as economy, quality, reliability and performance. These are known as economic motives, which are rational in nature, deal with the technical functions and performance of a product, and are usually expressed in quantitative terms.[4]

They can also be seen as the functional motives underlying buying behaviour. Physiological, emotional and economic motives are depicted in figure 4.4.

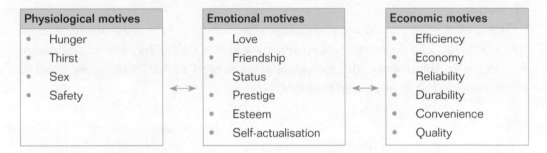

Physiological motives	Emotional motives	Economic motives
• Hunger	• Love	• Efficiency
• Thirst	• Friendship	• Economy
• Sex	• Status	• Reliability
• Safety	• Prestige	• Durability
	• Esteem	• Convenience
	• Self-actualisation	• Quality

Figure 4.4 Motives of consumers

Source: Adapted from Walters, GG. 1978. *Consumer behaviour.* Homewood: Richard D Irwin, p 53.

4.3.1.2   Perception

A motive activates behaviour intended to satisfy the aroused need. Since behaviour can take many forms, an individual gathers information from the environment to help in making a choice. The process of receiving, organising and assigning meaning to information or stimuli detected by the five senses is known as *perception.* It is the way that consumers interpret or give meaning to the world surrounding them. The consumer can, for example, form a perception of the quality of a product by feeling it or by just looking at it.

Perception involves seeing, hearing, feeling, tasting and smelling. Stimuli picked up by the senses are relayed to the brain, where they are interpreted. The consumer reacts according to this interpretation and not always according to the objective reality. Subjective factors always play a role in perception. The experiences, values and prejudices of an individual colour his or her perceptions. This means that few people perceive things in exactly the same way.

Sensory stimuli

- *Seeing* plays a role in purchasing jewellery and fashion clothes.
- *Hearing* plays a role in purchasing musical instruments and electronic equipment.
- *Feeling* plays a role in purchasing material/clothes, fruit and bread.
- *Tasting* plays a role in purchasing sweets, toothpaste and foodstuffs.
- *Smelling* plays a role in purchasing perfume, fresh bread, flowers and deodorants.

In purchasing a new car, all the senses except taste play a role in perception.

Consumers must pick up sensory stimuli from the environment before they will react. Perception also plays a role in the interpretation of a marketing message. Consumers will perceive a certain market offering only after they have received sensory stimuli, especially after seeing or hearing the marketing message.

Because so many, often conflicting, stimuli are perceived simultaneously, individuals tend to defend themselves. They may ignore or distort the meaning of unwelcome stimuli. Such perceptual defence mechanisms[5] are used to protect a person against undesirable stimuli from the environment, and include the following:

- *Selective exposure* occurs when people selectively choose to expose themselves only to certain stimuli. A consumer can, for example, avoid unwelcome stimuli by quickly paging through a magazine and missing the advertisements or by turning off the radio or television when commercials come on.
- *Selective attention* occurs when the individual does not pay full attention to the stimuli picked up by the senses. Selective attention causes a consumer not to comprehend the content of the marketing message.
- *Selective interpretation* occurs when the stimuli are perceived, but the message itself is not interpreted as it was intended to be. The consumer can interpret the marketing message incorrectly by distorting the meaning or by misunderstanding it.
- *Selective recall* refers to the individual's ability to remember only certain stimuli and to forget others which may be important. At the point of purchase, consumers may have forgotten the advertisement and must therefore once again be reminded to purchase the product (see figure 4.5).

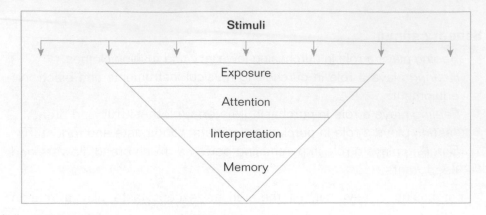

Figure 4.5 Information processing is selective

Source: Cant et al. 2006. M*arketing management.* Cape Town: Juta, p 80.

A marketing manager may find different ways to deal with the following:

1. Selective attention

- Larger stimuli (one-page advertisements versus fractional advertisements) and higher frequency (the repetition of advertisements on the radio or in different media) will be more likely to be noticed.
- Both colour and movement attract attention.
- Objects placed near the centre of the visual field are more likely to be noticed than those near the edge of the field (eye-level space in supermarkets).

2. Selective interpretation

- Marketers should carefully pretest their message to ensure that it is being interpreted correctly.
- Marketers should determine how cultural differences influence the use of colour, symbols and numbers.
- Marketers should not set unrealistic expectations.

3. Selective retention

- Visibility influences the ability to retrieve items from our memory for use in consumption decisions (in this case, it would assist to make use of demonstrations).
- Repetition is important to reinforce the message.
- Make use of the consumer's ability to learn (the result of a combination of motivation, attention, experience and repetition).

Source: Bennett, JA, Grove, TA & Jooste, CJ. 1995. *Introduction to marketing management.* Johannesburg: RAU internal publication, pp 35–36.

4.3.1.3   Learning ability

The consumer's ability to learn also influences behaviour. The consumer must, for example, learn which product attributes relate to which brand and where it can be purchased. Consumers must also be able to recognise the distinctive packaging. Consumers must remember the information supplied in the marketing message when they are in a position to purchase the product.

Learning can be defined as the result of a combination of motivation, attention, experience and repetition. Three elements are implied in this definition. In order to learn, the learner/consumer must be *motivated* and give *full attention* to the message (must perceive and experience it), and there must be some measure of effective *repetition.* A considered combination of these three elements results in a successful learning situation. Imbalance in any way invariably leads to failure.[6]

The following learning principles are important when formulating marketing messages:

- Repetition is important to reinforce the message.
- A unique message is best remembered.
- A message which is easy to understand is easy to learn.
- The law of *primacy* states that the aspect mentioned at the beginning of the message is best remembered, but according to the law of *recency,* the last-mentioned aspect is best remembered.
- Demonstrations facilitate the learning process.
- Promises of rewards (or threats of punishment) facilitate learning.
- Serious fear-producing messages are avoided; consumers tend to distort such messages.

4.3.1.4   Attitude

An attitude is a positive or negative feeling about an object (e.g. a brand, product or company) that predisposes a person to behave in a particular way toward that object.[7] Attitudes also encompass an individual's value system, which represents personal standards of good and bad, right and wrong, and so forth.[8]

Negative attitudes to products

- Conservationists abhor killing wild animals and maintain a very negative attitude to the wearing of fur coats.
- Members of some religious groups disapprove of the use of cosmetics or eating beef and/or pork.
- Conservative people exhibit a negative attitude towards unconventional fashions. They often forbid their children to purchase such items.
- Some men may have negative attitudes towards using diet soft drinks which they believe are targeted primarily at women.

All attitudes have the following in common:

- Attitudes are learned through previous experience with a product or indirect experiences such as reading about the product or interaction with social groups.
- Attitudes relate to an object – consumers can hold attitudes only about something, and they will vary from object to object.
- Attitudes have direction and intensity. Attitudes toward the object are either favourable or unfavourable. The consumer either likes or dislikes diet soft drinks. The strength of their liking or disliking can also differ – some customers may like the object more than others do.
- Attitudes tend to be stable – once formal, attitudes usually endure, and the longer they are held, the more resistant to change they become.

Marketers strive to reinforce positive attitudes held by consumers. The Toyota Camry is seen as a spacious and economical family car. The advertising campaign reinforces these attitudes by emphasising the boot space or the fact that three children can comfortably fit on the back seat.

It is far more difficult to change strongly held attitudes. When a marketer is faced with negative or unfavourable attitudes, there are various options:[9]

- Change the consumer's beliefs about the attributes or brands, for example the campaign to promote red meat as healthy is endorsed by the Heart Foundation.
- Change the importance of beliefs. For years, consumers have known that bran cereals are high in natural fibre. Today, however, these cereals are promoted as a possible factor in preventing certain types of cancer.
- Add new beliefs, for example that a particular toothpaste not only prevents tooth decay but also whitens teeth, or a washing powder that brightens the colour of a garment.

4.3.1.5 Personality

Personality refers to individuals' unique psychological makeup, which consistently influences how they responds to their environment. Personality distinguishes one individual from another, and one group of individuals with similar characteristics from another group.[10] There are several personality types identified by research.

While research seems to indicate that individual traits are not good predictors of behaviour, it is a well-known fact that marketers use personality traits to describe individuals and to differentiate between them. (See table 4.2 for examples of traits.) It is also true that marketers can expect that consumers will tend to purchase the product that best suits their personality. Mercedes-Benz drivers are, for example, perceived to be more conservative than BMW users, who are perceived to be far more aggressive and assertive.

Table 4.2 Examples of personality traits

Reserved (critical, stiff)	vs	**Outgoing** (warm-hearted, participating)
Humble (stable, mild)	vs	**Assertive** (aggressive, competitive)
Self-assured (secure, complacent)	vs	**Apprehensive** (insecure, troubled, worrying)
Relaxed (tranquil, composed)	vs	**Tense** (frustrated)
Expedient (disregards rules)	vs	**Conscientious** (persistent, moralistic)
Dependent (follower)	vs	**Self-sufficient** (resourceful, independent)
Undisciplined (lax, careless)	vs	**Controlled** (willpower, precise, comprehensive)

Source: Hawkins, D; Best, RJ & Coney, KA. 1995. *Consumer behaviour.* Chicago. Richard & Irwin, p 310.

4.3.1.6 Lifestyle

Lifestyle refers to the way of living of individuals or families. The lifestyle concept provides descriptions of behaviour and purchasing patterns, especially the ways in which people spend their time and money. Personality, motives and attitudes also influence lifestyle.

The AIO classification describes lifestyle according to the activities, interests and opinions of consumers. Figure 4.6 indicates some dimensions of lifestyle which can be used to describe the attributes of a specific market segment. Market segmentation is discussed in chapter 5.

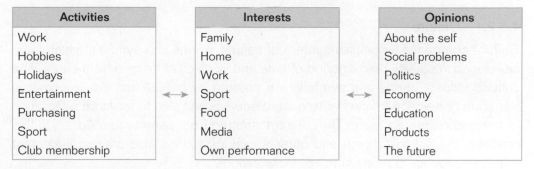

Activities	Interests	Opinions
Work	Family	About the self
Hobbies	Home	Social problems
Holidays	Work	Politics
Entertainment	Sport	Economy
Purchasing	Food	Education
Sport	Media	Products
Club membership	Own performance	The future

Figure 4.6 Lifestyle dimensions
Source: Cant et al. 2006. *Marketing management.* Cape Town: Juta, p 84.

Examples of South African lifestyle groups as identified by the South African Advertising Research Foundation (SAARF) are as follows:

* Good living
* Sports lovers
* Gamers
* Traditionalists
* Homebodies
* Outdoors
* Gardeners
* Showgoers
* Bars & betters

4.3.2 Group factors influencing consumer buying decisions

The consumer is a human being who needs to be affiliated with other groups in the social environment in order to satisfy social needs. Group norms will therefore influence the individual's behaviour patterns. These norms include habits, rules and regulations.

Sanctions (rewards or punishment) are used in formal and informal ways to ensure conformity to norms. Rewards such as social acceptance and approval encourage a person to conform to the prescribed norms of behaviour. Sanctions (such as ostracism) are usually regarded as a very serious punishment by most people. Subtle threats of this nature are often included in advertisements for toothpaste, deodorants and skin lotions, the implication being that the person not using these products is in danger of being ridiculed, held in contempt or ostracised.

Considering the fact that an individual can belong to many different groups (all of which maintain distinctive norms of behaviour), one can appreciate the degree of social pressure placed on the economic activities of an individual. There are very few products that are without any social significance at all, and usually a consumer succumbs to the pressure of social needs. The different groups that can compel a consumer to conform to group norms are the cultural group, the family, reference groups and option leaders.

4.3.2.1 Culture

Culture comprises a complex system of values, norms and symbols which have developed in society over a period of time and in which all its members share. The cultural values, norms and symbols are created by people and are transmitted from one generation to another to ensure survival and also to facilitate adaptation to the circumstances of life. They are transmitted from parents to children. In this process, the school, church and other social institutions also play an important role (this process is referred to as *socialisation*).

Each cultural group comprises several subcultures, each with its own norms, values and symbols. There are four main subcultures, categorised according to nationality, religion, race and geographical area of residence. Besides the four main groups, smaller subcultures can develop, perhaps according to language, age, interests or occupation.

South African society is fragmented into many cultural groups and subgroups. Although whites are not numerically dominant, their norms, values and symbols do exert influence on economic activity. Most advertisements therefore reflect Western culture. Advertising messages are directed simultaneously at the black and the white consumer markets, and are often variations on the same theme. Marketing management must, however, be careful not to use symbols which can be interpreted incorrectly (or differently), and not to portray unacceptable behaviour patterns. Effective communication can take place only if the theme of the advertising message reflects the cultural norms, values and symbols of the cultural group to which it is directed.

4.3.2.2 Family[11]

Of all the groups influencing consumer behaviour, the individual maintains the closest contact with the family. In family interaction, the child learns behaviour patterns by means of the socialisation process.

The family can be regarded as a nuclear group whose members live in close contact with one another and act as a decision-making unit when they attempt to satisfy individual needs from one shared source (the family income). This fact implies that individual needs must necessarily be subordinated to those of other members to a greater or lesser extent. This leads to consultation and joint decision making among family members.

With regard to the influence of the family, there are two aspects which are of importance to the enterprise in developing its marketing strategy: the family life cycle and role differentiation between family members. The family life-cycle phases are as follows:

- *Newlywed phase.* Both members of this unit are usually economically active and pool their incomes, which means they can usually afford to buy durables and even luxuries.
- *Phase of* family *growth.* This phase starts with the arrival of the first child in the relationship, and markedly changes previous consumer behaviour patterns.
- *Maturity phase.* The children in the family have reached the adolescent stage where, in addition to their basic needs, they have also developed their own norms, preferences and lifestyles.
- *Post-parental phase.* All the children have left home, and the parents spend proportionally less on basic household necessities. They have greater disposable income to spend on luxuries.
- *Sole survivor.* One spouse dies, and the consumption patterns and the lifestyle of the surviving spouse change drastically.

Role differentiation and the influences exerted by family members on consumer decision making in the family are depicted in table 4.3.

Table 4.3 Role differentiation in consumer decision making in the family

Roles	Family members
The **initiator** is the person who makes the first suggestion regarding products to be purchased.	Teenagers often act as initiators, for example requesting a soft drink or ice cream. ⮕

Roles	Family members
The **influencer** is the person who implicitly or explicitly influences the final decision because this person's suggestions and wishes are reflected in the ultimate decision made by the family.	Children's preferences (e.g. for a certain kind of breakfast cereal) influence family decision making.
The **decision maker** is the person who actually chooses between alternatives and makes the decision.	This is usually the mother or the father.
The **purchaser** purchases the products.	It is usually the mother's responsibility to purchase the groceries.
The **user** is the person who actually uses the products.	The baby consumes the vegetable purée purchased by the mother.

Source: Adapted from McDaniel, C & Darden, WR. 1987. *Marketing*. Boston: Allyn & Bacon, p 146.

4.3.2.3   Reference groups

Individuals may belong to many sorts of groups. A group consists of two or more people who interact with each other to accomplish some goal. Examples include families, close personal friends, co-workers, members of an organisation, leisure and hobby groups, and neighbours. Any of these groups may become reference groups.

A reference group involves one or more people that a consumer uses as a basis for comparison or 'point of reference' in forming responses and performing behaviours.[12] In all reference groups, there are distinctive norms of behaviour, and members are expected to conform to them in order to avoid sanctions being applied against them.

The following types of reference groups influence consumer behaviour patterns:

- *Membership groups* are groups to which the person has obtained membership, for example friends or a social club.
- *Automatic groups* are groups to which a person belongs purely as a result of age, sex or occupation. A peer group is an example of an automatic group.
- *Negative groups* are groups with which a person does not wish to be associated. A person intentionally avoids the norms of the negative group; examples are smokers or drinkers.
- *Associative groups* are those groups to which a person aspires to belong, for example a group with higher status or level of acceptance among peers, or those of celebrities or sports stars.

Typical members of associative reference groups are often used as models in advertisements in order to show potential consumers the type of person who buys the product and also the way in which the product can be used.

The advertising message attempts to persuade potential customers to follow the example set by these models. Members of perceived negative groups can also be used in advertising; for example overweight models in health-food advertisements.

Reference groups affect consumer behaviour in three ways:

- *Normative influence.* Norms of behaviour are laid down by the reference group, and group members behave accordingly (they wear the same type/ brand of clothes or shop at the same retail store).
- *Value – expressive influence.* Behaviour portrays certain values, for example health consciousness, environmental consciousness or ethical behaviour.
- *Informational influence.* Consumers often accept the opinions of group members as credible, especially when it is difficult to assess product or brand characteristics by observation.[13]

Reference group influence can extend to the decision to purchase a product as well as the choice of a specific brand. Bearden and Etzel[14] indicate the following situations where strong reference group influence occurs:

- *Publicly consumed luxuries.* There is a strong influence on decision to buy product and the choice of the brand (e.g. cellphones).
- *Privately consumed luxuries.* There is a strong influence on decision to buy product but not on brand (e.g. water purifiers).
- *Publicly consumed necessities.* There is a strong influence on brand choice (e.g. wrist watches).
- *Privately consumed necessities.* There is no reference group influence (e.g. underwear or mattresses).

4.3.2.4 Opinion leaders

The opinion leader has an important function in the marketing communication process, acting as a go-between in what is known as the two-step flow of communication. Research results have indicated that information does not flow directly from the mass media to individual consumers in the target market but is channelled through a person, the *opinion leader,* who interprets and evaluates the information, relaying acceptance or rejection of the message to other consumers in the target market.

The role of the opinion leader is especially important in purchasing high-risk new products. In the case of a new fashion, for example, the fashion opinion leader is willing to accept the risk of ridicule or financial loss, which the ordinary consumer is usually anxious to avoid. The latter will only become interested after the new fashion has been vetted and approved by the opinion leader. This process of gradual acceptance is known as *diffusion.*

There is a great deal of overlap between leader and follower roles. Every consumer is a member of several different reference groups and is influenced by these groups as well as by the opinion leaders in them. In the same way, one person can be an opinion leader in one group while being a follower in another. The marketer must identify the relevant reference groups and the opinion leaders as this will ensure the effective communication of the advertising message and the acceptance of this message by the target market.[15]

4.4 The buying decision-making process

When buying products, consumers follow a decision-making process, as shown in figure 4.8. Not all consumers proceed in order through all the steps. Consumers engaged in extensive decision making go through all the steps. Each of the steps in the decision-making process will be discussed briefly.

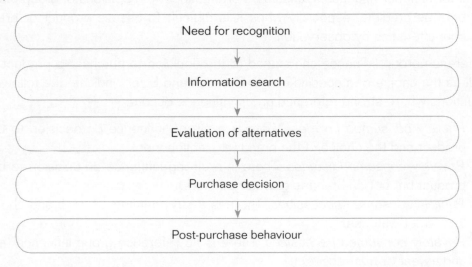

Figure 4.8 Stages of the purchase-decision process

4.4.1 Need for recognition

The process by which a consumer makes a purchase decision begins when the consumer recognises a need. This phase is sometimes called the *problem recognition* or *problem awareness* phase. When an individual perceives a difference between the desired state of affairs and the actual state of affairs, an unsatisfied need is felt or recognised. A problem exists which must be dealt with as soon as possible. The recognition may come from an internal stimulus such as hunger or fatigue, or a desire to impress people. Alternatively, it may come from external stimuli such as an advertisement, the launch of a new product or an invitation to a party.

Marketing managers can, without any doubt, make consumers aware of unsatisfied or even dormant needs. It must be emphasised, however, that marketing messages cannot convince a person of unfelt needs, and cannot persuade consumers against their will.

Other reasons for consumers becoming aware of a need that can be satisfied by buying a specific product are:

- the availability on the market of a new, improved product;
- a change in the consumer's circumstances (e.g. more or less money is available to spend);
- out-of-stock situations (a person buying groceries once a month); and
- dissatisfaction with the product currently in use.

4.4.2 Information search

After consumers have identified a need, they may then look for information about how best to satisfy it. Whether the consumer does or does not search for more information depends on the perceived benefits of the search versus the perceived costs. The perceived benefits include finding the best price, obtaining the most desired model and achieving ultimate satisfaction with the purchase decision. The perceived costs include the time and expenses of undertaking the search. Consumers will spend time and effort searching as long as the benefits of the search outweigh the costs.

Depending on how much experience a consumer has in meeting a particular type of need, the consumer will seek information from the following sources:[16]

- *Internal sources.* There is information lodged in the person's memory. For routine purchases or those made out of habit (e.g. shampoo), this may be the only source of information.
- *Group sources.* The consumer often consults with other people (family, friends and colleagues). These sources of information may be the most powerful in shaping purchase decisions, especially where the consumer is inexperienced or uncertain.
- *Marketing sources.* Consumers obtain information from marketers, through salespeople, advertisements, product displays and packages.
- *Public sources.* These are sources independent of the marketer, for example reports in the media or ratings by independent organisations or individuals.
- *Experiential sources.* The consumer may also experience the product while shopping, for example by handling it, tasting it, smelling it or trying it out.

From all these sources the consumer usually identifies several alternatives to satisfy the need. The set of alternatives that the consumer identifies is known as the *consideration* or *evoked set*. The products or brands in the evoked set are those which the buyer can further evaluate. For example, there are more than 200 models of cars available, yet many consumers consider only four or five different models.

The extent to which an individual conducts an external search depends on the following factors:

- *Perceived risk.* The higher the risk the more extensive the search.
- *Knowledge level of the buyer.* The better informed the consumers are, the less they need to search for information.
- *Prior experience.* Buyers with no prior experience in buying a certain product will spend more time seeking information.
- *Level of interest in the product.* A consumer who is more interested in a product will spend more time searching for information.[17]

4.4.3 Evaluation of alternatives

Evaluation entails the appraisal by the consumer of the attributes and benefits of various alternatives. A host of criteria may be used to evaluate products.

The abundance of evaluation criteria involved in any major decision makes evaluation very difficult indeed. The decision maker must also decide on the relative importance of often conflicting criteria. In table 4.4 some product and psychological criteria which can be applied in the evaluation of alternatives are given.

Table 4.4 Evaluation criteria

Product criteria	Psychological criteria
Cost/price	Satisfaction of social needs
Quality/durability	Satisfaction of ego needs
Aesthetic qualities (e.g. colour, style and texture)	Image of product (or store)
	Contribution of the product to lifestyle

Some of the criteria in table 4.4 can be evaluated in an objective way. Price, quality and performance standards of alternatives can be compared objectively, but personal and subjective factors play an important role in the evaluation of aesthetic qualities, the image of the product and the contribution of the chosen item toward need satisfaction and lifestyle. In the evaluation of alternative points of purchase (stores), the evaluation criteria may include the product assortment, hygiene considerations, the image projected by the store, and the conduct of the sales personnel.

Evaluation takes place in the mind of the consumer and is an example of covert behaviour. One cannot actually see someone weighing the alternative attributes of various products and those which have led to the final decision, Consumers are often unwilling to acknowledge that psychological criteria play an important role during the evaluation phase.

The perceived risks associated with buying a specific product also impact on the evaluation process. Table 4.5 shows which risks are critically evaluated by a consumer during evaluation,

From table 4.5 it can be deduced, for example, that older people with a low income, experiencing ill health and suffering from anxiety caused by loss of self-esteem, status and affiliation with others will probably be sensitive to most risk factors. It will be difficult for them to make a decision to purchase.

Table 4.5 Risk factors considered during evaluation

Type of risk	Typical consumer	Type of product
Financial risk	Consumers with inadequate funds, with a low income or those sensitive to financial loss	Expensive products, e.g. homes and cars
Functional risk	Practical people for whom the functional aspects of products are deemed important	Appliances requiring a degree of dedication, e.g. computers and microwave ovens
Physical risk	Older and disadvantaged people and those for whom health and vitality have high priority	Mechanical products which can cause injuries, as well as health products and medicine
Social risk	Individuals aiming to prove themselves and those that lack self-confidence	Symbolic products, e.g. fashion clothing, jewellery, sporting equipment and deodorants
Psychological risk	Individuals who have a strong need for respect and status	Expensive personal luxuries

Source: Solomon, MR. 1994. *Consumer behaviour*. Boston: Allyn & Bacon, p 228.

4.4.4 Purchase decision

After searching and evaluating, the consumer must decide whether to buy or not. If the decision is to buy, a series of related decisions must be made, for example:

- brand decision;
- vendor decision;
- quantity decision;
- time decision; and
- payment method decision.

Table 4.6 contains a summary of these decisions.

Table 4.6 Where, how much, when and how consumers purchase

Consumer decision making			
Where?	How much?	When?	How?
Supermarket	Purchases regularly	Time of day	Cash
Discount store	Purchases now and then	Day of the week	On credit
Department store		Beginning of season	Lay-by
Shopping centre	Purchases never		Hire purchase

Source: Cant et al. 2006. *Marketing management*. Cape Town: Juta, p 70.

4.4.5 Post-purchase behaviour

After purchasing the product, the consumer will experience some level of satisfaction or dissatisfaction. The marketer's job does not end when the product is bought, but continues into the post-purchase period.

Marketers must monitor post-purchase satisfaction, post-purchase actions and cognitive dissonance.

4.4.5.1 Post-purchase satisfaction[18]

What determines whether the buyer will be highly satisfied, somewhat satisfied or dissatisfied with a purchase? The buyer's satisfaction is a function of the closeness between the buyer's product expectations and the product's perceived performance. If the product's performance falls short of customer expectations, the customer is disappointed; if it meets expectations, the customer is satisfied; if it exceeds expectations, the customer is delighted. These feelings make a difference in whether the customer buys the product again, and discusses the product favourably or unfavourably.

Consumers form their expectations on the basis of messages received from sellers, friends and other information sources. If the seller exaggerates the benefits, consumers will experience unfulfilled expectations, which leads to dissatisfaction. The larger the gap between expectations and performance, the greater the consumer's dissatisfaction. Here the consumer's coping style comes into play. Some consumers magnify the gap when the product is not perfect and they are highly dissatisfied. Other consumers minimise the gap and are less dissatisfied.

4.4.5.2 Post-purchase actions

The consumer's satisfaction or dissatisfaction will influence future behaviour. A satisfied consumer will purchase the product again and spread positive messages about the product. Dissatisfied consumers will respond differently. They may stop using the product or return it, or they may take some form of public action.

4.4.5.3 Cognitive dissonance

In making a final choice, the consumer had to forego other attractive options, and also had to part with money (perhaps a great deal of it), which could have been used for other purposes. It is no wonder, therefore, that the consumer often develops doubts regarding the wisdom of the decision. This negative feeling of doubt and uncertainty in the post-purchase period is referred to as *cognitive dissonance*,[19] a negative emotion stemming from a psychological inconsistency in the cognitions (the things that a person knows).

Dissonant consumers will try to correct these psychological inconsistencies by attempting to convince themselves that the original decision was correct and very judicious. In order to do so, they may rationalise by putting forward logical reasons for decisions taken and may also turn to others for approval and reassurance.

The post-purchase evaluation phase can be regarded as the beginning of a new decision-making process. Will the consumer consider repurchasing the same product? Routine decision making develops when a brand-loyal consumer insists on purchasing the same brand every time,

4.5 Business buying behaviour

Businesses buy goods and services for the following purposes:

- To manufacture other goods and services (e.g. raw material, equipment, components and tools).
- To resell to other organisational buyers or to consumers (e.g. retailers or wholesalers).
- To conduct the organisation's operations (e.g. office equipment, stationery and cleaning materials).

These products are bought according to planned and structured purchasing procedures by trained and well-informed buyers employed by the organisations. The buyer is not only knowledgeable about the enterprise's requirements but has also consulted and analysed outside sources of information. The buying decision is usually taken by more than just one person and is based on rational considerations. This is in contrast with consumer decisions, which are often based on the satisfaction of psychological and social needs.

The following issues regarding organisational buying behaviour will be discussed in section 4.5.1:

- How organisational buying behaviour differs from the consumer buying behaviour.
- The buying decisions that buyers make.
- The participants in the buying process.
- How industrial buyers make their buying decisions.

4.5.1 Differences between organisational and consumer buying behaviour

The following are the unique characteristics of organisational buying behaviour:

- There are usually more people involved in the purchasing process, each with a specific role to play.
- The process is often technically more complex.
- Buyers acquire products for further production, for use in operations, or for resale to final customers.
- The purchase process tends to focus more on rational needs.
- The post-purchase process is often more significant, for example the need for service and installation.

- There is a greater interdependency between buyer and seller as long-term relationships evolve.
- Buyers are more likely to have unique needs that require customised manufacturing to specifications.
- More personal selling is involved as both parties hammer out the details.
- Decisions are often more time consuming (products are complex and a greater number of individuals are involved).
- Buyers must follow policies and compare guidelines which place restrictions on what and from whom they can buy.[20]

4.5.2 Types of buying decisions[21]

The organisational buyer faces a set of decisions in making a purchase. The number and nature of the decisions depend on the buying situation. Four types of buying decisions can be distinguished:

- *New-task buying.* This is the most difficult and complex buying situation because it is a first-time purchase of a major product, for example a computer system, production machinery or custom-built offices. Typically, several people are involved in the buying decision because the risk is great. Information needs are high and the evaluation of alternatives is difficult because the decision makers have little experience with the product. Marketers have the challenge of finding out what the buyers needs are and to communicate the product's ability to satisfy them.
- *Straight rebuy.* This is a routine, low-involvement purchase with minimal information needs and no great consideration of alternatives. It is usually handled by the purchasing department, who simply chooses from approved suppliers on its list. Suppliers who are not on this list may have difficulty with initial contact with the buyer. Examples are the repeat purchase of office supplies, chemicals, small components, and bolts and nuts.
- *Modified rebuy.* This buying situation is somewhere between the other two in terms of time and number of people involved, information needed and alternatives considered. In a modified rebuy, the buyer wants to modify product specifications, prices, terms or suppliers and needs to evaluate suppliers on a regular basis. Examples are buying a new truck, personal computers, consulting services or components.
- *Systems buying.* Some buyers prefer to buy a packaged solution to a problem from a single supplier. This practice began with governments buying major weapons and communication systems. Instead of buying components and assembling the machinery, buyers ask for bids from suppliers who would supply the components and assemble the package or system. Spoornet, for example, strives to produce a package of logistic services (transport, warehousing, insurance and shipment) to their key clients.

4.5.3 Buying centre

The decision-making unit of a buying organisation is called its *buying centre. A* buying centre can be defined as all the individuals and units that participate in the decision-making process. The size and makeup of the buying centre will vary for different purchases and for different buying situations. The individuals also differ in terms of their authority, the status of their positions, their credibility and their degree of empathy.

The members of the buying centre can play any of the following roles:

- *Users* of the product or service include those people who usually initiate the act of purchasing and play an important role in defining the various purchasing specifications. Users can influence buyers' actions negatively (by, for example, refusing to use a particular supplier's product) or positively (by, for example, using a new product that is more cost effective).
- *Influencers* are all those who have a direct or indirect influence on the purchasing decision, for example engineers involved in the design of product specifications or the evaluation of alternatives.
- *Buyers* are those who have the authority to select suppliers and sign contracts.
- *Decision makers* are those concerned with the approval of transactions. In the case of routine purchases, the buyer usually makes the decision, but in the case of unique and important purchases, senior management usually approves the transaction.
- *Gatekeepers* are those individuals in the business who control the flow of information from one person/department to another person/department, for example restricting salespeople from making direct contact with users or influencers.

In analysing the buying centre, a marketer strives to answer the following questions.

- Who are the individuals that form the buying centre?
- What is each member's power base?
- What is each member's relative influence in the decision?
- What are each member's evaluation criteria and how does he or she rate each prospective supplier on these criteria?

4.5.4 Buying decisions

The organisation buying process consists of the following eight stages:

- *Problem recognition* – recognising a problem or need.
- *General need recognition* – describing general characteristics and quantity of needed item.
- *Product specification* – specifying the best technical product specifications.
- *Supplier search* – trying to find the best supplier.

- *Proposal solicitation* – inviting qualified suppliers to submit proposals.
- *Supplier selection* – reviewing proposals and selecting a supplier.
- *Order routine specification* – writing the final order, and listing technical specifications, quantity needed, delivery time, return policies, warranties and so on.
- *Performance review* – rating satisfaction with suppliers, and deciding whether to continue, modify or stop them.

Buyers facing a new-task buying situation would probably go through all the stages of the buying process. Buyers making modified or straight rebuys will usually skip some of the stages in the buying process. See table 4.7 for an indication of the steps in each buying situation.

Table 4.7 Influence of buying situations on buying decisions

Buying stages	Buying situations		
	New buy	**Modified rebuy**	**Straight rebuy**
Problem recognition	Yes	Maybe	No
General need recognition	Yes	Maybe	No
Production specification	Yes	Yes	Yes
Supplier search	Yes	Maybe	No
Proposal solicitation	Yes	Maybe	No
Supplier selection	Yes	Maybe	No
Order routine specification	Yes	Maybe	No
Performance review	Yes	Yes	Yes

Summary

In this chapter, the focus was firstly on the individual consumer and the factors influencing consumer behaviour. Individual as well as group determinants influencing the decision-making process were described.

The chapter concluded with an overview of organisational buying behaviour. It described the different decisions that buyers make, the participants in the decision-making process and the buying decisions.

In the next chapter, the emphasis falls on the various segments in the market. Marketing management direct its marketing offering to chosen segment(s) as it is improbable that all needs can be satisfied with a single market offering.

References

1. Kotler, P & Armstrong, G. 1994. *Principles of marketing.* Englewood Cliffs, NJ: Prentice Hall, p 171.
2. Assael, H. 2004. *Consumer behaviour and marketing action.* Boston: Kent, pp 96–100.

3. Kotler, P & Keller, KL. 2006. *Marketing management.* Englewood Cliffs, NJ: Prentice Hall, p 200.
4. Cant, MC, Brink, A & Brijball, S. 2006. Cape Town: Juta, pp 138–139.
5. Kotler et al, pp 185–186.
6. Kotler et al, pp 186.
7. Cant et al, pp 122–123.
8. Boyd, HW, Walker, OC, Mullins, J & Larreche, J. 2001. *Marketing management.* Boston: Irwin, p 125.
9. Lamb, CW, Hair, JF & McDaniel, C. 2006. *Marketing.* Cincinnati: South Western College Publishing, p 175.
10. Blackwell, RD, Miniard, PW & Engel, JF. 2001. *Consumer behaviour.* Cincinnati: South Western, p 212.
11. Cant, MC, Strydom, JW, Jooste, CJ & Du Plessis, PJ. 2006. *Marketing management.* Cape Town: Juta, pp 86–87.
12. Assael, p 400.
13. Blackwell et al, p 398.
14. Bearden, WO & Etzel, MJ. 1982. Reference group influence on product and brand purchase decisions. *Journal of Consumer Research*, September, p 185.
15. Cant et al. *Marketing management*, p 89.
16. Churchill, GA & Peter, JP. 1995. *Marketing: Creating value for customers.* Boston: Irwin, pp 249–250.
17. Lamb et al, p 145.
18. Kotler & Keller, p 198.
19. Blackwell et al, pp 80–81.
20. Kotler & Keller, pp 210–211.
21. Kotler & Keller, p 212.

CHAPTER FIVE

Market segmentation, targeting and positioning

Learning outcomes

After you have studied this chapter you will be able to:

- explain the concept of market segmentation;
- indicate how marketers can segment their market;
- highlight the prerequisites for effective market segmentation;
- explain what is meant by the term 'target marketing';
- suggest factors that should be considered when selecting a target market;
- explain the concept of product positioning;
- discuss the positioning process; and
- describe the positioning methods that marketers can pursue in practice.

5.1   Introduction

In an ever-changing market environment with competitors entering at will due to the greater global market, the growth of the market and the consumer needs and wants, fewer resources and more demands from consumers, it is becoming increasingly important that companies regularly evaluate their own position and decide on the market strategy to follow. This implies that they have to reflect on the markets they are currently in or intend servicing, and to segment the market accordingly. In order to be successful, marketers need to satisfy the demands of the customer, and the more specifically they meet these demands, the greater the chances of success. In order to meet their primary objective, however, companies must make a profit. This is the reason why segmentation is needed – that is, to identify those segments which are economically viable and will result in profit for the company.

Marketers are quick to realise that to satisfy an individual customer's need is not economically feasible – it is far too costly and unrealistic. Instead, marketers need to generalise about the needs, demands and preferences of the heterogeneous market, at the same time realising that they cannot be all things to all people – they must focus on satisfying a specific market's needs and concentrate on what they do best to remain competitive in an increasingly cutthroat marketplace. How this can be achieved is the central theme of this chapter.

5.2 Segmentation, targeting and positioning defined

In order to survive over the long term, it is imperative that a company meets the needs of the target market it has selected to serve. It is not good enough to keep on doing the same things all the time, as needs change and companies must adapt to this. It is therefore essential that marketers constantly monitor the segments they are serving for any changes or new demands that may arise. If they do not, their competitors will. Although the satisfaction of customer needs is not a goal in itself, it enables the enterprise to achieve its own goals. Therefore, the greater the need satisfaction customers can derive from an enterprise's products, the easier it becomes for the enterprise to achieve its own goals. To achieve maximum customer satisfaction, marketers therefore divide the heterogeneous market into fairly homogeneous subsets of customers. This process is referred to as *market segmentation.* Each segment of the market, it is assumed, will have similar needs, and will respond in a similar way to the market offering and strategy. The market for clothing, for example, can be subdivided into the following sub-segments: babies, girls, boys, teenagers, maternity, petite, men's and outdoor clothes. Each of these segments exhibits different characteristics and needs with regard to occasion, usage, fashion and so forth. It follows that no single garment can cater for all the unique needs of all these market segments.[1]

The organisation must decide next which market segment(s) needs it can best satisfy. The Business Express train service (Gautrain) that runs between Pretoria and Johannesburg has, for example, decided to cater primarily for the needs of the business commuter, and has therefore developed its product offering around this segment. The process of deciding which segment(s) to pursue is referred to as *market targeting.*

Once the target market segment has been selected, the company must decide how to compete effectively in it. A decision has to be made concerning the competitive advantage to be achieved. This is known as *positioning.* A company can decide to compete on the basis of a lower price (when compared to competitors), or on the basis of ambience and value, which would be reflected by the quality of the merchandise, the layout of the store, the store design, the prices charged and the availability of services required by customers. Alternatively, it may decide to compete on the basis of a superior range of clothing items and location. The discussion in this chapter centres on these core concepts.

5.3 Segmenting the market

Segmenting the market is a crucial task as the future of the company is dependent on the correct identification of the market to serve and the correct basis on which the market is segmented. This refers, among others, to the following issues with regard to market segmentation: firstly, the advantages and disadvantages of market segmentation; secondly, the prerequisites of effective market segmentation;

and lastly, the common bases used to segment consumer and industrial markets concludes. Let us look at these issues in more detail.

5.3.1 Advantages and disadvantages of market segmentation

Market segmentation offers the following advantages to marketers:

- Firstly, it forces marketers to focus more on customer needs. In a segmented market, the marketer can fully appreciate the differences in customer needs, and respond accordingly. A greater degree of customer satisfaction can be achieved if the market offering is developed around customer needs, demands and preferences.
- Secondly, segmentation leads to the identification of excellent new marketing opportunities if research reveals an unexplored segment. Without proper segmentation, such a market segment may remain untapped for years.
- Thirdly, market segmentation provides guidelines for the development of separate market offerings and strategies for the various market segments.
- Lastly, segmentation can help guide the proper allocation of marketing resources.

A large, growing market segment may be allocated a greater proportion of the marketing budget, while a shrinking one may be scaled down or eventually abandoned if it becomes unattractive.

However, market segmentation also has the following disadvantages which must be considered by the marketer:

- The development and marketing of separate models and market offerings is very expensive. It is much cheaper, for example, to develop only one product for one segment than to develop multiple products for multiple segments and multiple strategies
- Only limited market coverage is achieved, since marketing strategies would be directed at specific market segments only.
- Excessive differentiation of the basic product may eventually lead to a proliferation of models and variations and finally *cannibalisation*. Cannibalisation occurs when one product takes away market share from another developed by the same enterprise.

5.3.2 Prerequisites for market segmentation

The main aim of segmentation is basically to enhance customer satisfaction and the profitability of shareholders. To subdivide the market for small delivery vehicles into Western Cape and KwaZulu-Natal farmers would make little marketing or business sense. In this case, geographic location makes no difference since the requirements of the farmers remain the same regardless of location. Geographic location would be very effective as a means of segmenting the market for insecticides, since farmers in the Western Cape have to deal with different insects than the farmers in KwaZulu-Natal do. For market segmentation to be effective, it must meet the following criteria:

- *It must be measurable.* If it is not possible to measure the size, purchasing power, potential profit and profile of the segment, it would be extremely difficult to compare such a segment with others, or to properly assess its attractiveness.
- *It must be large enough.* Pursuing a market segment that is too small is not profitable. A segment must be the largest homogeneous group of people worth exploiting with a tailored market offering and marketing strategy. Although South Africa boasts a large variety of cultures, some of them, such as the Chinese community, may be so small that they do not warrant special attention by marketers.
- *It must be accessible.* Marketers must be able to reach the market segment with their market offering and strategy. How is it possible, for example, to reach rural people if they cannot read or do not listen to the radio? Such a segment is largely inaccessible to the marketer.
- *It must be actionable.* It must be possible to develop separate market offerings for different market segments. Smaller enterprises are often unable to develop different market offerings or marketing strategies, even if they realise that there are distinct differences between various segments.
- *It must be differentiable.* Different market segments must exhibit heterogeneous needs. In other words, people in different segments must have different needs, demands and desires. People in the same segment, on the other hand, must exhibit similar characteristics and needs. The marketer should also be able to distinguish the segments from each other without too much difficulty.[2]

Once marketing management is satisfied that a specific segment conforms to these conditions, it can be considered as a possible target market.

5.3.3 Bases for segmenting consumer markets

5.3.3.1 Variables used in segmentation

The marketing manager can utilise different variables to segment a market. These variables can generally be classified according to *geographic, demographic, psychographic* and *behaviouristic* bases. Table 5.1 provides a detailed analysis of these classification bases.

Table 5.1 shows the bases for segmenting consumer markets in the first column, while the different variables that can be used for each are shown in the second column. In the following sections we offer a brief explanation of each approach.

Table 5.1 Bases for segmenting consumer markets

Bases	Possible variables
Geographic	
Region	Gauteng, Durban-Pinetown, Cape Peninsula, KwaZulu-Natal, Northern province
Size of city or town	Under 10 000, 10 000–20 000, 20 000–25 000, over 25 000 inhabitants
Density	Urban, suburban, rural
Climate	Summer rainfall, winter rainfall, very hot and humid, very hot and dry
Demographic	
Age	Under 7, 7–13, 14–19, 20–34, 35–49, 50–65, 66+
Gender	Male, female
Family size	1 and 2, 3 and 4, more than 4 members
Family life cycle	Young married couples without children; young married couples with children; older married couples with children; married couples without children living in; single
Annual income	Under R20 000, R20 001–R50 000, R50 001–R80 000, R80 001–R110 000, R110 001–R140 000, R140 001–R170 000, over R170 000
Occupation	Professional and technical, managerial, clerical, sales and related services, farmers, students, housewives, unemployed, retired
Religion	Protestant, Catholic, Muslim, Hindu, Jewish
Race	White, black, coloured, Asian
Education	Grade 10, Grade 12, diploma, degree, postgraduate
Psychographic	
Lifestyle	Conservative, liberal
Personality	Gregarious, authoritarian, impulsive, ambitious
Social class	Upper, middle, lower
Behavioural	
Purchase occasion	Regular use, special occasion
Benefits sought	Economy, convenience, prestige, speed, service
User status	Non-user, ex-user, potential user, regular user
Usage rate	Heavy user, medium user, regular user
Loyalty status	None, medium, strong, absolute
Readiness stage	Unaware, aware, informed, interested, desirous, intending to buy
Attitude to product	Enthusiastic, positive, indifferent, negative, hostile

Source: Adapted from Kotler, P & Keller, KL in Cant, MC, Strydom, JW, Jooste, CJ & Du Plessis, PJ. 2006. *Marketing management*. Cape Town: Juta, p 108.

The following three factors are important:

1. A mutual relationship may exist between some of these bases. It is possible, for example, that there is a strong relationship between income, occupation and education on the one hand, and between family size and geographic region on the other. In the tourism industry, for example, there is a strong relationship between income, occupation and education, and the likelihood of travel.[3]

2. Needs seldom relate to one segment base only. A specific marketing strategy is unlikely to be directed only to people with an income of R15 000 to R20 000 per year. A better description of a particular market segment often utilises more than one segment base, for example unmarried women between 21 and 30 years of age with an income of more than R60 000 per year and living in the Gauteng area.

3. The market segmentation bases described in table 5.1 are not complete. In the tourism industry, for example, marketers also use distance travelled, trip purpose, buyer needs and benefits sought as segmentation bases. The number of possible segmentation bases is to a great extent determined by the creativity of the marketing manager.

5.3.3.2 Geographic segmentation

In segmenting a market geographically, the marketer divides the total market into different geographical areas, such as countries or regions. Variations such as the size of the city or town or population density may also be appropriate bases. The enterprise can then decide to target only one or a limited number of geographical areas. If customers in different areas exhibit diverse needs, these differences can be addressed at local level.

Until the late 1980s, population density was thought to be a good predictor of consumer behaviour and needs. With the advent of black taxi operators during the late 1980s and the beginning of the 1990s, this has become an increasingly poor predictor, since more and more rural black people travel to the major cities and metropolitan areas to do their shopping.

In a fairly small geographic area such as Johannesburg, marketers realise there are diverse markets, such as the central, southern, northern, western and eastern areas of Johannesburg, that can be treated as separate market segments with diverse needs. Many smaller entrepreneurs have decided to confine their marketing and operations to only one or two of these segments.

5.3.3.3 Demographic segmentation

Demographic segmentation is probably the most common base for segmenting consumer markets. This may be because of the relative ease with which the approach can be applied, or because consumer needs are often strongly associated with these variables.[4]

Traditionally, companies in South Africa, with its diverse population groups and cultures (as explained in greater detail in a previous chapter), used race heavily as a basis for market segmentation. The majority of research reports or business plans published during the 1970s and 1980s distinguished between the needs of black, white, coloured and Asian consumers. Increasingly, however, companies are moving away from this approach, making more use of other segmentation variables such as income, education, lifestyle, living standards, and so on.

In 1993, the South African Advertising Research Foundation (SAARF) published its first Living Standards Measure (LSM) report, explaining how it arrived at eight LSM categories, using 13 variables such as degree of urbanisation and ownership of cars and major appliances instead of the outmoded category of race.[5]

Since then the SAARF LSM has become the most widely used marketing research tool in South Africa. The most recent LSM classification divides the population into ten LSM groups, 10 (highest) to 1 (lowest). In table 5.2 we provide a brief description of the of the LSM groups. (The Internet contains more information on the LSM.)

It should be noted that, even in the 1990s, culture and religion remained powerful segmentation bases, primarily because the different cultures and religions have vastly different traditions, beliefs, taboos and preferences which must be accommodated. Differences include the languages that people speak, the food they eat, the clothes they wear, and the sport they watch or participate in, to mention only a few.

Table 5.2 Description of selected LSM groups

Brief description of LSM 1–10	
LSM 1: 4,8% of adult population	**LSM 2: 11% of adult population**
Demographics	**Demographics**
Females between the ages of 16 and 24, or 50+. Completed primary school and live in rural areas, mostly in a traditional hut. Their average household income is R1 058 per month	Females between the ages of 16 and 24. Completed primary school and live in rural areas mostly in a house or matchbox house. Their average household income R1 261 per month
Media	**Media**
Radio is a major channel of communication Commercial radio – mainly African language services	Radio: Commercial radio – mainly African language services
General	**General**
Minimal access to services Minimal ownership of durables, except radios	Water on plot Minimal ownership of durables, except radios and stoves
LSM 3: 11,9% of adult population	**LSM 4: 14,4% of adult population**
Demographics	**Demographics**
Aged 16–34. Schooling up to some high school and live in rural areas mostly in a house or matchbox house. Their average household income is R1 613 per month	Aged 16–34. Schooling up to some high school. Their average household income is R2 022 per month
Media	**Media**
Radio: Commerical radio – mainly African language services, Ukhozi FM, Umhlobo Wenene FM TV: SABC1 Outdoor advertising	Radio: Commerical radio – mainly African language services, Metro FM TV: SABC1, SABC2, etv Outdoor advertising

General	General
Electricity and water on plot Minimal ownership of durables, expect radios and stoves Activities: Buying lottery tickets	Electricity, water on plot, and flush toilet TV sets, hi-fi/radio set, electric hotplates, fridge Activities: Stokvel meetings, buying lottery tickets, buying and eating takeaway food
LSM 5: 13.9% of adult population	**LSM 6: 16% of adult population**
Demographics	**Demographics**
Males between the ages of 16 and 34. Completed up to matric and live in urban areas. Their average household income is R2 903 per month	Males between the ages of 25 and 34. Completed up to matric and higher. They live in urban areas. Their average household income is R4 723 per month
Media	**Media**
Radio: Commerical – mainly African language services stations, Metro FM. TV: SABC1, SABC2, SABC3, etv Daily/weekly newspapers and magazines Outdoor advertising	Wide range of commercial and community radio stations. TV: SABC1, SABC2, SABC3, etv Daily/weekly newspapers and magazines Outdoor and cinema advertising
General	**General**
Electricity, water on plot, and flush toilet TV sets, hi-fi/radio set, stove, fridge Activities: Exercising, painting interior of house, stokvel meetings, purchasing takeaway food and lottery tickets	Electricity, hot running water and flush toilet Ownership of a number of durables plus a cellphone Participate in a number of activities
LSM 7: 8,5% of adult population	**LSM 8: 6,2% of adult population**
Demographics	**Demographics**
Males between the ages of 35 and 49. Completed up to matric and higher. They live in urban areas. Their average household income is R7 579 per month	Males 35+ years that have completed up to matric and higher. They live in urban areas. Their average household income is R10 015 per month
Media	**Media**
Wide range of commercial and community radio stations TV: SABC1, SABC2, SABC3, etv, M-Net and DStv Access to the Internet Daily/weekly newspapers and magazines Outdoor and cinema advertising	Wide range of commercial and community radio stations TV: SABC1, SABC2, SABC3, etv, M-Net and DStv Access to the Internet Daily/weekly newspapers and magazines Outdoor and cinema advertising
General	**General**
Full access to services Increased ownership of durables plus a motor vehicle Participation in all activities	Full access to services Full ownership of durables incl. DVD, PC and satellite dish Participation in all activities
LSM 9: 7,2% of adult population	**LSM 10: 14,8% of adult population**
Demographics	**Demographics**
Males 35+ years that have completed up to matric and higher They live in urban areas Their average household income is R13 500 per month	Males 35+ years that have completed up to matric and higher They live in urban areas Their average household income is R20 278 per month

Media	Media
Wide range of commercial and community radio stations.	Wide range of commercial and community radio stations.
TV: SABC2, SABC3, etv, M-Net and DStv	TV: SABC2, SABC3, etv, M-Net and DStv
Access to the Internet	Access to the Internet
Daily/weekly newspapers and magazines	Daily/weekly newspapers and magazines
Outdoor and cinema advertising	Outdoor and cinema advertising
General	**General**
Full access to services	Full access to services
Full ownership of durables including DVD, PC and satellite dish	Full ownership of durables including DVD, PC and satellite dish
Participation in all activities excluding stokvel meetings	Participation in all activities excluding stokvel meetings

Source: Adapted from SAARF. 2008. [Online]. Available from: http://www.saarf.co.za/LSM/LSM2008.zip

5.3.3.4   Psychographic segmentation

Psychographic segmentation involves the segmentation of the market by means of categories such as social class, lifestyle or personality. To establish the different lifestyle categories, information concerning the respondents' attitudes, interests and opinions (A10), or values and lifestyles (VALS) is collected and then subjected to factor analysis to identify separate subgroups.

Locally, the ACNielsen MRA Sociomonitor value groups survey is the most authoritative psychographic profile of its kind in South Africa. In order to create the value groups, respondents answer an extensive battery of psychographic statements. Their answers are then grouped and scored, giving every single respondent a different score and position on the 'social map', depending on their answers.

These scores are then statistically analysed and the value groups – a broad groups of consumers with similar values, attitudes, and motivations (psychographics) – are established, The five value groups embrace the full spectrum of values among South African adults. They help marketers to understand what motivates their customers, and hence how best to appeal to them. The data can also aid marketers in more effective media placement.

Five value groups have been identified from the 1997 all-adult database. These are as follows:

1. Conformists (19,6% of all adults, or 5,042 million people).
2. Transitionals (20,5% of all adults, or 5,278 million people).
3. Progressives (18,8% of all adults, or 4,833 million people).
4. Non-conformists (17,0% of all adults, or 4,375 million people).
5. Today-ers (24,1 % of all adults, or 6,193 million people).

Table 5.3 contains a condensed profile of the five value groups, according to the latest Sociomonitor reports available from ACNielsen MRA.

Table 5.3 Sociomonitor value groups

Conformists (19,6% of the adult population, or 5,042 million adults)
This Value Group is characterised by conformity to group value systems. Traditions, religion, and the family and home are paramount. Probably because of their civil- and group-adhering values, they would like to see harmony between the different race groups, the South African nation as a whole, and the genders. They are accepting and understanding of others' emotions. Probably because of their strongly religious orientation, they are not comfortable with sexual liberty issues. They feel more secure within group norms than as individuals. They would rather be looked up to and accorded status for socially acceptable or civil behaviour than for materialistic reasons. Familiarity makes them most comfortable; they do not usually desire too much novelty, excitement or risk. As a result of their adherence to traditions and the familiar, they are typically not comfortable with new products and technology, and would probably need coaxing to change from the brands they use. Practicality comes before beauty – price and usefulness are the overriding factors in their purchase decisions.

Transitionals (20,5% of the adult population, or 5,278 million adults)
This Value Group is characterised by traditional values with some focus on personal achievement and thus the assumption of individualistic and more modern values. The more traditional values are group oriented, such as past orientation, *ubuntu*, familism, religion and cultural customs. Consequently, there is a strong group orientation, but a stronger need for novelty and self-achievement, and not always automatic acceptance of all authority, rules and/or group-oriented conventions. They take pride in their own achievements and are materialistic – it is important that others see what they have achieved. Despite their status and materialistic orientation, price consciousness and practicality prevail over aesthetics in their purchase decisions, As part of their self-focus, health and their looks are also important. Unlike the Conformists, the Transitionals are not too outward looking, and are slightly hardened to others beyond their immediate circles – so despite their softer traditional values, they are not as accepting of other races or individual choices as the Conformists are.

Progressives (18,8% of the adult population, or 4,833 million adults)
The Progressives are a modernised group whose primary needs are self-development but also some harmony in acquiring meaning from and giving back to the group. They are proudly focused on self-improvement and development of every aspect of their personal lives – so they like to take care of, enhance and project beautiful physical looks, their health and home environments, and want to acquire new skills to stimulate their mind. Quality and intrinsics are a primary need in everything they do, including purchasing. There is some materialism and a desire to show others what they have achieved or acquired. They are comfortable with new technology, but do not need novelty or sensation for excitement. Probably as part of their search for meaning, there is acceptance that they are part of a bigger picture, and therefore there is some embracing of traditional and religious norms. However, not all traditions are automatically adhered to if they are not relevant to their lives (e.g. they are below average in terms of familism, past orientation and African customs). There is also empathy with others' feelings.

Non-conformists (17,0% of the adult population, or 4,375 million adults)
This group rejects any group-oriented, civil, and/or traditional values in favour of individualism. They tolerate and accept other individuals easily, regardless of gender or race differences, and uphold their rights to individual choice. Non-conformists are drawn to technology and technological gadgetry – these are the people who take readily and comfortably to new technology. Nevertheless they are not materialistic for the sake of materialism, and shun the ownership of material goods merely to impress others. The goods that they acquire will be selected for their technological innovation and relevance to their lives. As part of their anti-establishment stance, they do not relate to conventional definitions of success and status. As individuals they have enough self-confidence to stand alone, so do not believe in making the effort to improve their looks or immediate surroundings, or furthering their education or skills, merely for the sake of it. They live their lives slightly on the edge – there is a tendency to want, or actually indulge in, raw thrills, fun and action rather than too much of the 'softer' self-development activities.

Today-ers (24,1% of the adult population, or 6,193 million adults)

Today-ers present a tough do-not-care exterior to the world. There is a strong rejection of anything resembling group civility or conventions. They are extrinsics oriented – they will buy on brand externals and lower price rather than intrinsics – and need to show off to others what they have and who they are. There is an inclination for thrills and action, and living on the edge. Stimulants and relaxants like alcohol and cigarettes, and maybe other drugs, and sex too, are used for sensation and escapism. There is little acceptance or tolerance for the rights to individual sexual choice or equality of the genders, and little feeling for or understanding of others, especially for those outside their relatively narrowly defined sense of who and what is acceptable. For all their rough-and-tough attitude, Today-ers have little to look forward to and have little self-confidence as individuals, hence the need for bolstering from their peer group. Despite being materially aspirational and extrinsics bound, they take little interest in self-improvement of any form. This probably has a lot to do with lack of opportunities, and consequently they feel disempowered and cannot relate to their personal part in improving their situation. This also means that they are generally out of touch with the latest technology or Western developments (and they tend to live more in the past than in the future).

Source: Adapted from ACNielsen MRA Sociomonitor 1997, 1999.

5.3.3.5 Behaviouristic segmentation

Buyers can also be segmented on the basis of their buying behaviour. This may take the form of the following:

Purchase occasions

Some buyers may use a product very regularly, while others may use it only on special occasions. Orange juice and champagne are two examples of products that fall into this category. Orange juice is often drunk mainly with breakfast, while champagne is mostly drunk on special occasions such as graduation, engagements and weddings. Consumption of these products can be increased by promoting the use of them at other occasions, such as lunches and dinners in the case of orange juice, or Valentine's Day in the case of champagne.

Benefits sought

Some market segments may be very specific in what benefits they seek when buying a specific product. Some may seek economy in a motor vehicle, while others may prefer speed or a good maintenance plan. When consumers are very specific with regard to the benefits they seek, marketers can respond with products that address these needs. In so doing, they satisfy their customers' needs.

User status

Consumers can be segmented into groups consisting of the non-users, ex-users, potential users or regular users. A balanced approach would require that an enterprise focus on both regular as well as potential users. While the regular users guarantee survival in the short to medium term, potential users who can be enticed to become users represent future growth.

Usage rate

Marketers can make provision for different market segments based on how frequently buyers buy their products. Heavy users should receive special attention by marketers, since they may represent the bulk of sales revenue. It is therefore common to see hotels, casinos and airlines develop special clubs or frequent flier programmes to appeal to this important segment of the market.

Loyalty status

Consumers vary in the degree of loyalty they have towards the organisation or its brand names. On the one extreme, one finds the switchers, or those consumers who show no loyalty toward any brand. They can be attracted through frequent sales, but it may sometimes not be worthwhile attracting them. On the other hand, there are very loyal buyers. Hardcore loyals would insist on a particular brand and would go to great lengths to acquire it. Ideally, they should be retained, and where possible they should be encouraged to become spokespeople for the organisations' products and services, as suggested by the relationship marketing philosophy.

Buyer readiness stage

Different marketing approaches have to be followed, depending on the consumer's readiness to buy. Potential consumers who are unaware of the product must first be made aware of it, while those who intend buying the product must be persuaded to do so. When cellphones were introduced to the South African market, most people were either unaware, or aware but not informed, of the product. Initially, awareness had to be established, and as it increased, more aggressive strategies were followed in the marketing of cellphones.

Attitude towards the product

By segmenting consumers according to their attitude towards the product, an enterprise can increase its marketing productivity.

Market segments that are negative or hostile towards a product can be avoided, saving valuable time and money. Attempts can be made to persuade those who are indifferent, while those who are enthusiastic or positive can merely be encouraged to support the product in future. Kotler (2006) quotes the political campaigner as an example in this regard. Hostile and negative voters are avoided, while the enthusiastic and positive ones are merely reminded to vote on election day. More time is spent with indifferent voters in order to persuade them to support a specific party.

5.3.4   Developing segment profiles

Every segment considered by the enterprise must be described fully with respect to its size, demographic and psychographic details, lifestyle, behavior patterns and product usage. Such a profile enables marketing management to develop products that will provide the need satisfaction utilities desired by customers and to design marketing communication messages that will appeal to these customers. In a later section, we provide practical hints on how to accomplish this.

5.3.5 *Bases for segmenting industrial markets*

Traditionally, industrial firms were reluctant to accept marketing segmentation as a marketing tool.[6] This can be attributed to the fact that industrial firms tend to be more engineering oriented, often focusing on product specifications rather than customer requirements. On the other extreme, one may find many industrial firms producing customised products or services to their customers. Consequently, they have no need to segment their market; they are producing for individual customers. Currently, the importance of market segmentation is increasingly realised by business-to-business marketers. Table 5.4 shows the most popular bases for segmenting industrial markets. It is clear that the marketer will consider totally different variables when segmenting the industrial market.

Table 5.4 Bases for segmenting industrial markets

Demographic
On which industries should we focus?
What size company must we target?
How many employees are in the organisation?
Which geographical areas must we target?
How long has the company been in business?
Does the company have one/multiple establishments?
Is it a local/national/international company?
Operating variables
On what technologies should we focus?
On what user types should we focus (heavy, medium, light, non-users)?
On what product types must we focus?
How frequently does the customer require delivery?
Should we focus on customers requiring many/few services?
Purchasing approaches
How centralised/decentralised is the purchasing function?
Should we focus on companies that seek quality/service/lower price?
Should we focus on companies that demand quick delivery/convenience/reputation/economy?
Should we focus on the companies with which we have strong links or should we target the most desirable ones?
Should we focus on those that prefer leasing/service contracts/systems purchases/sealed bidding?
Should we focus on organisations that are financial/marketing/production/engineering dominated?

Situational factors
Should we focus on customers who require quick and sudden delivery, or should we focus on those that require steady delivery?
Should we focus on specialised application of our product or on all applications?
Should we be focusing on small/medium/large orders?
Personal characteristics
Should we focus on companies who have similar values to ours?
Should we concentrate on risk takers or risk avoiders?
Should we focus on companies that show high loyalty towards their suppliers?

Source: Adapted from Cant et al. 2006. *Marketing management.* Cape Town: Juta, pp 124–125.

In particular, the marketer can employ the following bases:

5.3.5.1 Demographic dimensions

Any demographic dimensions such as company size, as reflected in the sales volume, number of employees or other criteria, geographical area, number of outlets or scope of operation (local/national/ international) can be used to classify companies into market segments.

5.3.5.2 Operational variables

Companies can also be classified according to their operational characteristics such as technology, user types, product types or frequency of delivery.

5.3.5.3 Purchasing approaches

Marketers of industrial products often have to negotiate with the purchasing departments of other businesses. It would therefore make sense to segment the market along these dimensions. Among the most important variables to be used is the degree of centralisation/decentralisation of the purchasing function, the power structure of the companies, the nature of the existing relationship with the customer, the purchasing criteria employed by the company, and so on. In a centralised purchasing department, for example, the buyer is more likely to consider all transactions with suppliers on a global basis, to emphasise cost savings and to minimise risks. A decentralised purchasing department will, on the other hand, be more concerned with the user's need, will tend to emphasise product quality and prompt delivery, and is likely to be less cost conscious.[7]

5.3.5.4 Situational factors

Criteria such as the delivery requirements of customers, the product application or the order size are regarded as situational factors. Often the marketer will find that about 80% of sales will be to customers who order in large quantities, while only about 20% will be to customers that buy in smaller quantities. The needs and demands of these segments will often vary greatly, justifying segmentation along these lines.

5.3.5.5 Personal characteristics

Marketers may also choose to segment the industrial market on the basis of the organisational values, risk profile or loyalty towards suppliers. Customers who are loyal to their suppliers can, for example, be treated with less aggression by salespeople, while the salesperson will have to be more aggressive in an attempt to retain the less-loyal market segments. It is also advisable to spread one's risk between risk takers and risk avoiders, which decreases the likelihood of a disaster.

As in the case of the consumer market, the industrial marketer must compile a comprehensive description of the characteristics, needs and demands of the various market segments, based on the criteria provided in this section. Figure 5.1 provides guidelines in this regard.

Firstly, it is necessary to identify the various market segments in the particular market. The manager must then list the characteristics of each of these segments. Thirdly, the marketer would derive the needs and preferences of each segment by studying their characteristics. Once this has been done, the product or service can be developed around the needs of the identified market segment(s).

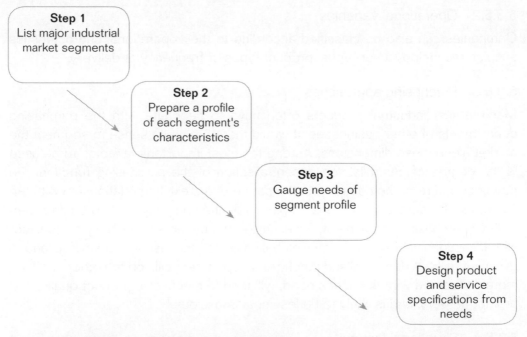

Step 1
List major industrial market segments

Step 2
Prepare a profile of each segment's characteristics

Step 3
Gauge needs of segment profile

Step 4
Design product and service specifications from needs

Figure 5.1 Compiling a profile of the industrial market
Source: Adapted from Cant et al. 2006. *Marketing management*. Cape Town: Juta, p 126.

This process allows the marketing manager to adapt his or her marketing strategy to the unique requirements of the targeted market segments. In an increasingly competitive business environment, this can only enhance the competitiveness of the enterprise.

5.4 Market targeting

After developing a comprehensive profile of the market segments based on the criteria indicated above, the next step is to decide to either target only one segment or a few, or even the whole market. This is referred to as *market targeting*. In this section, the focus is, firstly, on the criteria to be used to evaluate market segments and, secondly, on the approaches available to the enterprise.

5.4.1 Criteria for selecting potential target markets

Before a specific market segment is selected as a target market, it must first be evaluated according to five important evaluation criteria:

1. Segment size and growth possibilities

A target market need not necessarily be big. A small segment can often be more profitable than one in which a large sales volume can be realised.

Marketing management must be convinced that there are further growth possibilities, thus making the segment sustainable. The market for Rolex watches or Ferraris may be small but the profit potential is huge. This makes it a very attractive segment.

2. Attractiveness and potential profitability

The attractiveness of a target market lies not only in its size and growth possibilities, but also in the promise of long-term profitability. Attractive segments attract competitors, and intense competition can have a detrimental effect on future profits. Serious threats to attractive segments are aggressive competitors that can launch price wars or intensive advertising campaigns, or competitors who are able to develop new substitute products. The growing power of buyers and suppliers also threatens attractive target markets. If the threat is very serious, an enterprise that does have the necessary resources and skills can decide not to take the opportunity to select the segment as a target market.

A target market is generally attractive if it has some degree of interrelationship with other segments. Instead of serving a number of small segments, it would be much better to combine interrelated segments. Interrelationships exist among segments that use the same raw materials, similar production methods or joint distribution channels.

3. The resources and skills of the enterprise

Promising segment opportunities that do not fit in with the long-term objectives set by management cannot be utilised. The same applies when resources and skills to exploit the opportunity are lacking. A segment can only be chosen as a target market if marketing management is fully committed to serving this target market better than any other competitor does. This implies that the market offering must have an undoubted differential advantage to target market members. If not, it would be advisable to commit the cost and energy to an alternative option.

4. Compatibility with the enterprise's objectives

Apart from the resources and skills of the enterprise, the choice of a target must also consider the compatibility with the objectives of the enterprise. If it is found that the objectives of the enterprise cannot be enhanced by the choice of a particular market segment, it should be disregarded.

5. Cost of reaching the target market

When a potential target market is inaccessible to an enterprise's marketing strategies, or the cost to reach it is too high, it should not be considered.[8]

In order to assess the potential of each of the market segments identified during the segmentation process, Walker et al[9] propose five steps, as shown in figure 5.2. These steps are highlighted briefly in the following sections. The evaluation of potential market segments starts with the selection of a set of criteria which can be used to assess, firstly, the attractiveness of the particular target market and secondly, the competitive position of the enterprise with regard to a specific market segment. Because not all evaluation criteria are of equal importance, these factors are then weighed to reflect the relative importance of each.

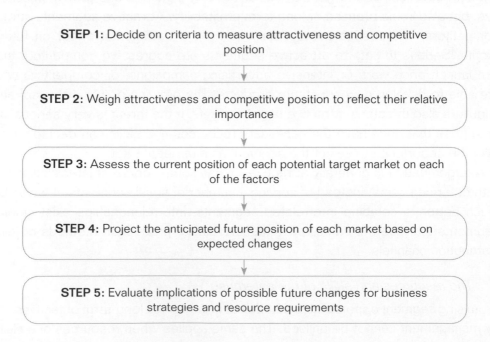

Figure 5.2 Steps in the evaluation of potential market

Adapted from Walker, OC, Boyd, HW & Larreche, JC in Cant et al. 2006. *Marketing management.* Cape Town: Juta, p 130.

The enterprise would then rate every market segment considered by the enterprise. Scores that reflect the market attractiveness and competitive position of the enterprise are then posted on a market attractiveness/business position matrix. Such a matrix is shown in figure 5.3. Once this has been done, the marketing manager will consider likely future changes that might manifest themselves. The arrow of segment A in figure 5.3 shows that this segment is expected to become less attractive in the future, while the organisation also believes that its competitive position will deteriorate. It is critically important to consider likely future changes, since the choice of a particular target market commits the enterprise to this market. Should changes occur in the future, the competitive position of the enterprise may be adversely affected.

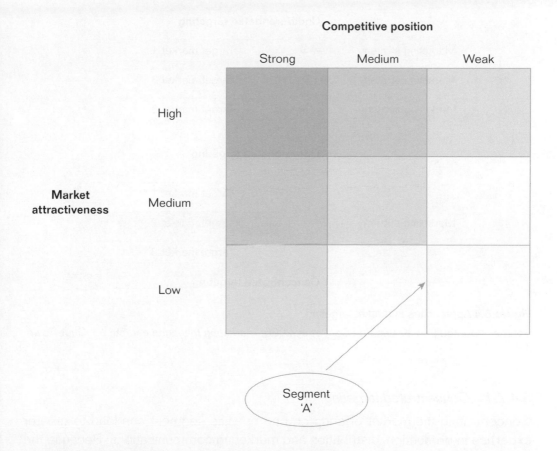

Figure 5.3 Market attractiveness/business position matrix

Source: Adapted from Walker, OC, Boyd, HW & Larreche, JC in Cant et al. 2006. *Marketing management,* 5th ed. Cape Town: Juta.

Given these possible changes, the marketing manager will lastly evaluate the implications of possible future changes with regard to their impact on company strategies and resource requirements. Only once this has been completed will the marketing manager finally choose a market segment or segments to target.

5.4.2 *Targeting market segments*

Marketers may choose one, two or multiple market segments to target. In essence, marketers can choose between three broad segmentation approaches to the market: *concentrated targeting, differentiated targeting* and *undifferentiated targeting.* Figure 5.4 reflects these approaches.

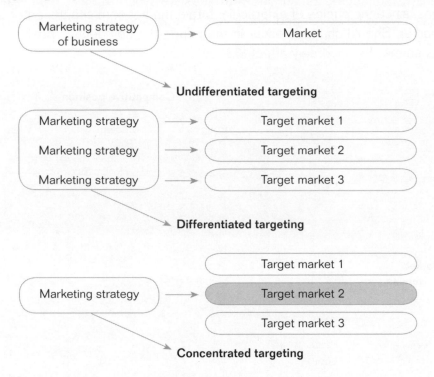

Figure 5.4 Approaches to market targeting

Source: Adapted from Kotler, P in Cant et al. 2006. *Marketing management,* 5th ed. Cape Town: Juta.

5.4.2.1 *Concentrated targeting*

Concentrating the market offering on one specific segment can lead to greater expertise in production, distribution and marketing communications. Because the product offering is aimed at one market segment only, it would be fair to argue that the enterprise will also be able to achieve greater customer satisfaction in this singular market segment. A big disadvantage, however, is that all efforts are then concentrated on one source. The risk of product failure and non-acceptance of the product is thus concentrated in a single target market. Should the preferences of the target market change, or should competitors enter the market with an improved offering, the enterprise may find itself without any business.

5.4.2.2 Differentiated targeting

In differentiated market segmentation, the enterprise elects to target two or more market segments, developing a unique marketing strategy for each one. This strategy allows the organisation to cater for the diverse needs of the different segments. It is, however, a costly strategy. In order to cater for the diverse needs, the enterprise incurs extra production costs as production runs become smaller, advertising costs rise because communication strategies must be adapted for the different market segments, administrative costs will increase as separate marketing plans have to be developed, and inventory costs go up as a greater variety of products must be maintained.

5.4.2.3 Undifferentiated targeting

When an undifferentiated marketing strategy is employed (also known as the *aggregation strategy*), the enterprise chooses to ignore the differences that are found in the market. Instead, they pursue the total market with one basic market offering. In practice, the enterprise would concentrate on the commonalities of the market segment rather than on the differences. One of the major advantages of such a strategy is the economies of scale that can be achieved with a standardised product and marketing strategy. This strategy has lost ground in recent years, as consumers have become more discriminating. Refer to figure 5.4 for an illustration of concentrated targeting, differentiated targeting and undifferentiated targeting.

5.5 Product positioning

The ultimate aim of the marketing actions of marketers is to position their products or services in the mind of their customers in a way that they want the customers to perceive them – that is, as a reliable supplier, a value-for-money product, a quality product, etc. Product positioning, therefore, refers to the way customers perceive a product in terms of its characteristics and advantages, and its competitive positioning. It thus involves the creation, in the minds of the targeted buyers, of a distinctive position with regard to the organisation's product relative to those of competing organisations. For positioning to be effective, it is important that the marketer understands customer buying criteria and recognises the performance of each competitor on each of the evaluative criteria.

5.5.1 Product positioning maps aid decision making

Marketers often use positioning or perceptual maps to portray market positions visually. A perceptual map is a multidimensional graphic image depicting consumer perceptions. These maps assist marketers in developing focused marketing mixes or strategies. It also helps the manager to assess the advantage of an organisation's marketing programme.[10]

Figure 5.5 offers an example of a positioning map for South African luxury motor vehicles. The map shows how consumers perceive the various models. The closer a model lies to a particular variable, the more that model is associated with this variable. There are various gaps on the map where no model is shown. Gaps like these are referred to as *competitive gaps*, and may indicate ideal marketing opportunities for the enterprise. However, marketers must proceed cautiously: these gaps may exist because it may be technically impossible to fulfil this requirement, or because it is an undesirable position due to limited customer interest.

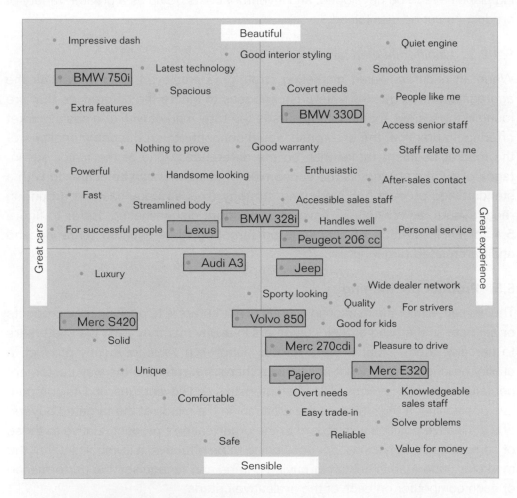

Figure 5.5 Positioning map for luxury vehicles in South Africa

Source: Supplied by Toyota SA.

Many other variables or determinants, such as those listed later in this chapter, can be used to compile similar positioning maps. However, marketing information and sophisticated statistical testing is necessary for the development of positioning maps.

5.5.2 *The positioning process*

A seven-step approach can be adopted when positioning brands. (The term 'brands' is preferred here since it is individual producers' brands not products that compete against each other in a market. Positioning maps can, however, also be developed for product categories.) These steps are shown in figure 5.6 and are discussed in this chapter.[11]

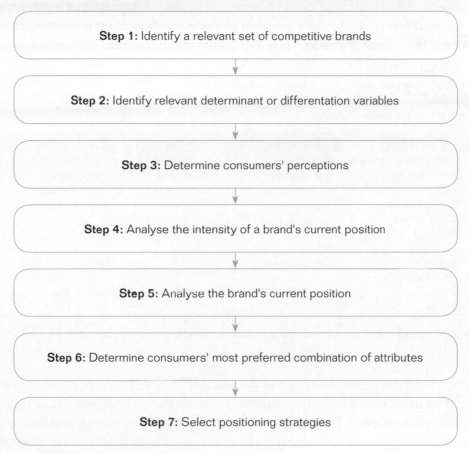

Figure 5.6 The positioning process
Source: Adapted from Walker, OC, Boyd, HW & Larreche, JC in Cant et al. 2006. *Marketing management,* 5th ed. Cape Town: Juta.

5.5.2.1 Identify a relevant set of competitive brands

The positioning process starts with the identification of a relevant set of competitive brands to which a particular producer's brand will be compared. It is essential that all relevant competing brands must be identified in order to make the positioning effort worthwhile. This enables marketers to identify the strengths and weaknesses of their own brand against a competing one. It also helps them to decide whether to reposition the brand in order to strengthen its position in the market. *Repositioning* refers to the changing of a brand's (mostly undesirable) position in the market in the hope that the new positioning will improve the brand's appeal among consumers.

5.5.2.2 Identify relevant determinant or differentiation variables

In essence, product positioning has to do with competitive differentiation and the effective communication of this to customers. Kotler[12] suggests that an enterprise or market offering can be differentiated along four different dimensions: product, services, personnel or image. Table 5.5 summarises the main differentiation variables suggested by Kotler. These are not the only variables that can be used, but the most obvious ones have been discussed.

Table 5.5 Differentiation variables

Product	Services	Personnel	Image
• Product features • Performance quality • Conformance to the target standard • Durability • Reliability • Repairability • Style • Design	• Delivery • Installation • Customer training • Consulting service • Repair • Miscellaneous	• Competence • Courtesy • Credibility • Reliability • Responsiveness • Communication	• Symbol • Media • Atmosphere • Events

Source: Adapted from Kotler, P in Cant et al. 2006. *Marketing management,* 5th ed. Cape Town: Juta.

The marketer must decide which of the above (or other) differentiation variables should be used in developing a positioning map. In this case, Walker et al[13] refer to *determinant variables.* They suggest that marketers must select those variables that play a major role in helping customers to differentiate among alternative brands in the market.

The following example serves to illustrate the importance of using determinant variables. Although safety is a major concern for all airline passengers, it is not regarded as a determinant variable as most customers use other features such as price, convenient flying times, service or frequent flier programmes to differentiate between competing airlines. Appropriate marketing research can aid the marketer in identifying determinant variables.

5.5.2.3 Determine consumers' perceptions

The marketer must establish how consumers perceive the various brands in terms of the determinant variables selected in the previous step. This step involves the collection of primary data from a sample of consumers. Using a structured questionnaire, these consumers (named respondents) are questioned about their perceptions of the various brands. The collected data is then analysed, using several statistical techniques. These include factor analysis, discriminant analysis, multidimensional scaling, and so on.

5.5.2.4 Analyse the intensity of a brand's current position

When a consumer is unaware of a brand, such a brand cannot clearly occupy a position in the mind of the consumer. In such instances, brand awareness must first be established. However, when a consumer is aware of a brand, the intensity of awareness may vary. In many markets, the awareness set for a particular product class may be as little as three or fewer brands when there are more than 20 brands in the product class. In such markets, the marketer of the lesser-known brand must attempt to increase the intensity of awareness by developing a strong relationship between the brand and a limited number of variables.

Competing directly with dominant brands is not advised. Instead, the marketer must identify as a target a position within a market segment that is not dominated by a leading brand. Alternatively, the marketer must concentrate on a variable that is highly prized by a particular market segment.

5.5.2.5 Analyse the brand's current position

From the data collected from consumers about their perceptions of the various brands in the market, the marketer can establish how strongly a particular brand is associated with a variety of determinant variables. To do this, a positioning map, similar to the one shown in figure 5.5, is developed. Brands that are close to each other on the map can be expected to be close rivals, while those that are far apart are considered very different from each other. Competitive rivalry between the latter is expected to be limited.

5.5.2.6 Determine consumers' most preferred combination of attributes

The discussion so far has focused on consumers' perceptions of existing brands and has not given any insight into the positions that would appeal most to consumers. This can be achieved by asking survey respondents to think of the ideal product or brand within a particular product category. Respondents would be asked to rate their ideal product and existing products on a number of determinant variables. The result of such an analysis of South African Airways (SAA) in the mid-1990s is shown in figure 5.7. The determinant variables that are closest to the ideal point are more important to consumers, while those that are further apart from each other are considered less important.

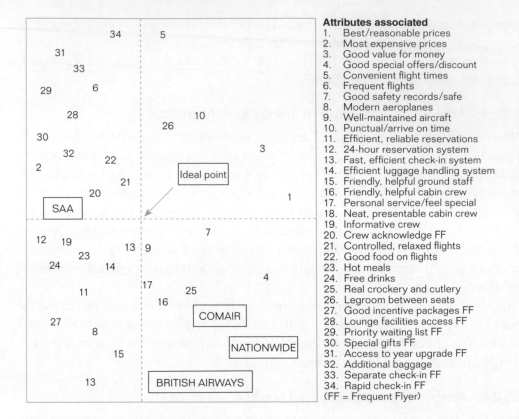

Attributes associated
1. Best/reasonable prices
2. Most expensive prices
3. Good value for money
4. Good special offers/discount
5. Convenient flight times
6. Frequent flights
7. Good safety records/safe
8. Modern aeroplanes
9. Well-maintained aircraft
10. Punctual/arrive on time
11. Efficient, reliable reservations
12. 24-hour reservation system
13. Fast, efficient check-in system
14. Efficient luggage handling system
15. Friendly, helpful ground staff
16. Friendly, helpful cabin crew
17. Personal service/feel special
18. Neat, presentable cabin crew
19. Informative crew
20. Crew acknowledge FF
21. Controlled, relaxed flights
22. Good food on flights
23. Hot meals
24. Free drinks
25. Real crockery and cutlery
26. Legroom between seats
27. Good incentive packages FF
28. Lounge facilities access FF
29. Priority waiting list FF
30. Special gifts FF
31. Access to year upgrade FF
32. Additional baggage
33. Separate check-in FF
34. Rapid check-in FF
(FF = Frequent Flyer)

Figure 5.7 Perceptual map of South African Airways based on ideal points

Source: Adapted from Louw, NS in Cant, MC (Ed). 2004. *Essentials of marketing*, 2nd ed. Cape Town: Juta.

5.5.2.7 Select positioning strategies

Deciding where to position a new brand or where to reposition an existing one depends on the market targeting analysis discussed earlier, as well as the market positioning analysis. The position chosen must reflect customer preferences and the positions of competitive brands. The decision must also reflect the expected future attractiveness of the target market and the relative strengths and weaknesses of competitors as well as the organisation's own capabilities. Specific positioning methods are discussed in the next section.

5.5.3 *Positioning methods*

In general, seven positioning methods can be distinguished:[14]

1. *Attribute positioning*

The enterprise positions itself in terms of one or more outstanding attributes. Benson & Hedges has chosen to position its cigarettes in terms of lightness and taste.

2. Benefit positioning

This positioning method emphasises the unique benefits that the enterprise or product offering offers its customers. For example, Gillette Contour blades promise a closer shave.

3. Use application positioning

An enterprise can position itself or its products in terms of the product use or application possibility, Graça, for example, is positioned as a wine to be enjoyed at all kinds of fun occasions.

4. User positioning

The enterprise may position their products with their users in mind. Marketers of bungee jumping can position their market offering to appeal to the thrill-seekers.

5. Competitor positioning

Some products can best be positioned against competitive offerings. BMW finds it useful to position its cars directly against those of Mercedes-Benz, its closest rival in South Africa.

6. Product category positioning

An enterprise can position itself in a product category not traditionally associated with it, thereby expanding business opportunities. A museum or planetarium, traditionally regarded as an educational institution, may elect to position itself as a tourist attraction.

7. Quality/price positioning

The enterprise may claim their product is of exceptional quality, or the lowest price. While Edgars is known for high-quality garments, Pep Stores is known for unbeatable prices.

After the marketer has decided on a particular positioning method, it must be communicated to the target market. Sun International has chosen to position its resorts as superior in quality. They employ all elements of the marketing strategy to communicate this quality image:

- The product itself reflects the positioning method to be used. Close inspection of the facilities, decor and ambience of the Lost City will confirm this.
- Price can be a strong indicator of quality, and the prices at Sun International reflect this.
- The efficiency of the distribution system (or central reservation system) can enhance the quality perception even further.
- The communication material about Sun International resorts reflects quality in the form of expensive paper, excellent photographs and layout (brochures),

professional radio advertisements and spectacular television advertisements.

Summary

Market segmentation remains one of the cornerstones of modern marketing. In this chapter, we defined the main theoretical concepts associated with market segmentation, targeting and positioning, and explained how it can be applied by marketers. It is imperative for those in marketing management to realise that they cannot hope to satisfy all markets. Instead, they must divide the heterogeneous market into more homogeneous groups of customers, choose one or more to target with their product offering(s), and position themselves relative to their competitors. Ultimately, the success of marketing management will depend on their ability to select profitable target markets in an ever-changing marketing environment, as well as their ability to satisfy the needs of the chosen segment(s).

References

1. Business Express. 2008. Business Express. [Online] http://www.sarcc.co.za/be.asp (accessed: 26 January 2009).
2. Kotler, P & Keller, KL in Cant et al. 2006. *Marketing management.* Cape Town: Juta, p 108.
3. Goeldner, CR, Ritchie, JRB & McIntosh, RW. 2000. *Tourism: Principles, practices, philosophies,* 8th ed. New York: John Wiley & Son.
4. Kotler, P & Keller, KL in Cant et al. 2006, op cit, pp 108–111.
5. South African Advertising Research Foundation. 2008. *The South African Advertising Research Foundation's living standards measure (LSM).* November.
6. ACNielsen MRA Sociomonitor 1997, 1999.
7. Cant, MC, Strydom, JW, Jooste, CJ & Du Plessis, PJ. 2006, op cit, p 122.
8. Kotler, P & Keller, KL. 2006. *Marketing management,* 12th ed. Upper Saddle River, NJ: Pearson Prentice Hall.
9. Cant et al. 2006, op cit, p 124.
10. Walker, OC, Boyd, HW & Larreche, JC in Cant, MC, Strydom, JW, Jooste, CJ & Du Plessis, PJ. 2008, op cit, p 126.
11. Walker et al in Cant et al. 2006, op cit, p 130.
12. Kotler, P & Keller, KL in Cant et al. 2006, op cit, p 132.
13. Walker et al in Cant et al. 2006, op cit, p 166.
14. Louw, NS in Cant, MC (Ed). 2004. *Essentials of marketing,* 2nd ed. Cape Town: Juta.

CHAPTER SIX

Integrated marketing

Learning outcomes

After you have studied this chapter you will be able to:

- explain how the marketing concept relates to the critical marketing decisions;
- explain how marketing information can be obtained through the marketing information system (MIS);
- explain the effect of the environment on the design of the marketing mix;
- discuss how the determinants of consumer behaviour influence marketing decision making; and
- identify how the choice of target market determines the design of the market offering.

6.1 Introduction

The previous five chapters established the core analysis and information sources that need to be identified, researched and discussed before any marketing decisions can be made. These core information areas form the basis for designing an informed and effective market offering. There is a strong tendency to discuss solutions or to prepare answers before the problem has been identified! In this chapter, we will establish how each of the previous chapters affects the decisions made by marketers in terms of offering a product or service to the marketplace. We will now establish the link between these core information areas and the market decisions.

In this chapter we will also investigate the process of trying to integrate the marketing effort to be able to compete effectively. For example, imagine trying to launch another cellular services brand in South Africa, with two giant entrenched competitors (Vodacom and MTN) to face. This was the situation facing Cell C when it launched its brand – and it has managed to gain about 14% of the market and turn a profit after seven years. The company achieved this by marketing innovative products and promotions to the mass market, weaving the elements of simplicity, choice and value into the makeup of the Cell C brand. It has integrated its communication and promotion efforts to establish a sustainable position in a very tough business environment.

6.2 The marketing process

Cant et al[1] explain that there are four major areas about which marketing management must make decisions. Once the target market is chosen, the marketer must make decisions about what to offer (*the product*), the place where the product is to be sold or delivered to the customer (*distribution of the product*), how the customer will be informed about the product (*marketing communications*) and the price of the product, which should reflect the value of the product to the customer. The four variables combine to represent the *market offering*, which the marketer develops in order to meet and satisfy the needs of the customer. These four variables (also known as the four Ps) make up the marketing mix.

Figure 6.1 shows how the core analysis and topics discussed in the previous chapters interact in the marketing process in order to facilitate the achievement of the enterprise's objectives. Once the target market is chosen and its needs properly understood through research, the marketing mix can be developed in order to meet the market needs. If this is done successfully, the marketer can contribute to the main objective of any business, namely the maximisation of profitability in the long term. This occurs within the context of a dynamic marketing environment.

Some authors[2] have questioned whether the traditional marketing mix (the four Ps) is an adequate one for the marketing of service products. They have proposed an expanded mix, which is more comprehensive and would also cover service products. The three elements added to the traditional mix to form this expanded mix are:

1. *Customer service.* This helps marketing management to differentiate the business, and helps to build closer relationships with customers.
2. *People.* The staff members form an integral part of the product, especially those employees who are involved in a high level of contact with customers.
3. *Processes.* The policies and procedures of the business influence how a product or service is created or delivered to customers.

Let us now examine each of the main components (and chapters) of this book and their relation to the marketing mix.

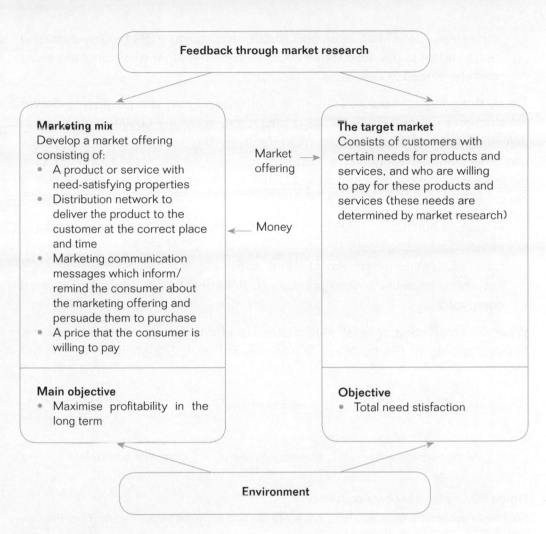

Figure 6.1 The marketing process

Source: Adapted from Cant et al. 2006. *Marketing management,* 5th ed. Cape Town: Juta, p 21.

6.3 Market orientation

A business that has a marketing orientation has three important characteristics:[3]

1. *Customer focus.* This refers to the efforts by the organisation to discover customer needs so that satisfaction can be delivered. Cell C focused on the mass market and tried to develop products that gave both value and choice to its customers, such as a R% recharge voucher called a "half tiger", and the Woza Weekend product that allowed free calls on weekends to other Cell C numbers.
2. *A team approach.* This refers to using cross-functional teams and an integrated approach to develop and deliver customer solutions.
3. *Competitor orientation.* This refers to a continuous recognition of where competitors have an advantage, and their competitive position and marketing

strategies. Cell C had been criticised for not having a 3G-type system, and had to adapt to the need in late 2008 because the other two competitors had well-developed 3G systems.

These three key characteristics lead to a business being in a position to deliver satisfaction to its customers. If this is measured, and if the business performs in delivering satisfaction to the customer effectively, the profitability of the business can be enhanced through better customer retention and increased loyalty. This is evidenced by the benefits that a loyal customer can ensure for a business over a period of time, which are:

- increased purchases;
- reduced operating costs;
- referrals to other potential customers; and
- the ability to justify a price premium to differentiate the product from price competitors.

When this marketing orientation is coupled to effectiveness in the marketplace, the profitability of the business is reinforced. Figure 6.2 shows this relationship.

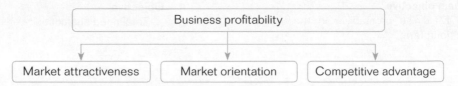

Figure 6.2 Drivers of business profitability

Source: Adapted from Best, RJ. 1997. *Market-based management.* Upper Saddle River: Prentice Hall, p 8.

Cant et al[4] summarise the effect of a strong marketing orientation by stating that the ultimate goal of this is to develop and implement marketing strategies that attract, satisfy and retain target market customers. This is done through the marketing strategy, which includes the target market and the marketing mix, as shown in figure 6.3.

Figure 6.3 Marketing orientation shapes marketing decisions

Source: Adapted from Best, RJ. 1997. *Market-based management.* Upper Saddle River: Prentice Hall, p 25.

Environmental change and marketing mix adaptation

In the late 1990s, Home Depot was the leading hardware and home improve-ments retailer in the US, but had found growth becoming slow and trading conditions difficult. As a result of research carried out, it found that about half of its purchases were made by women, and it had to reconsider its whole marketing mix in light of this. It responded by redesigning its shelv-ing and signage, softening the colour scheme inside its stores, improving its merchandise focus and choice, obtaining more proprietary brands, and changing the layout to make a better shopping experience for its customers. The changes added significantly to both turnover and profitability, as well as improving the shopping experience of its customers.

6.4 The marketing environment

In chapter 2 you learned that the marketing environment of a company is dynamic and made up of a number of sub-environments. What is important to remember is that the environment consists of a number of interacting influences. There are uncon-trollable variables, such as those that comprise the macro-environment (economic, political, social and technological). These can be contrasted with those variables under the direct control of marketing management, for example the marketing mix.

Marketing managers need to understand the wider business environment (macro-environment), but they should concentrate on those aspects which can be influenced, such as the controllable variables of product, price, communica-tion and distribution. Cant et al[5] point out that it is necessary to stress that the controllable variables are indirectly affected by these uncontrollable elements in the environment. The marketer must ensure that those variables that can be controlled reflect the realities of the uncontrollable variables in the marketing environment. This is illustrated in figure 6.4.

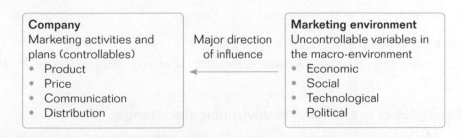

Company
Marketing activities and plans (controllables)
* Product
* Price
* Communication
* Distribution

Major direction of influence
←

Marketing environment
Uncontrollable variables in the macro-environment
* Economic
* Social
* Technological
* Political

Figure 6.4 Environmental influence
Source: Adapted from Cant et al. 2006. *Marketing management,* 5th ed. Cape Town: Juta, p 35.

The effectiveness of marketing will be determined by how well it can match the business's offerings to the requirements from the marketplace. Marketers will need to develop an outside-in orientation. This will be seen in the ability of the company to respond to changes in the environment, and is in effect the strategic role of the marketing function in the organisation.

This is not an easy task, as evidenced by the many organisations that have disappeared, or have lost market share to competitors. Many businesses become preoccupied with these daily operational problems (often termed 'firefighting') and tend to lose contact with the environment, often ignoring or discounting the small changes that are the precursors to more serious change.

Figure 6.5 illustrates a classic framework for environmental monitoring and adaptation, The environmental monitoring identifies short-term changes or long-term trends. These are translated into opportunities, threats or inconsequential events. If adaptation is required, it must be reflected in the controllable aspects of the marketing mix. In other words, the business must change something to respond to the change.

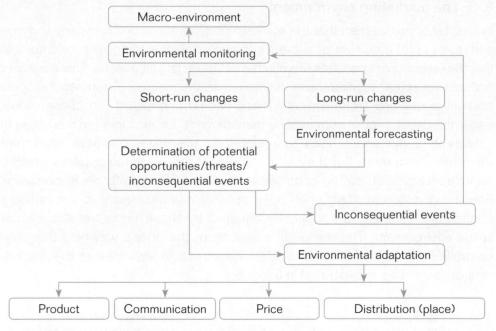

Figure 6.5 Environmental adaptation and monitoring

Source: Adapted from Busch, PS & Houston, MJ. 1985. *Marketing: Strategic foundations.* Homewood: Irwin, p 82.

Examples of responding to environmental change

- McDonald's latched on to the growing coffee demand in the US by launching a coffee product that added significantly to its bottom line – and which was recently voted best coffee in the US by a respected consumer-products rating organisation.

➲

6.5 Obtaining and using marketing information

The contents of chapter 3 should have convinced you that it is imperative for a marketing organisation to have an effective marketing information system (MIS). This system helps to integrate all the different types of marketing information and makes this information available to the decision makers in a useful and timely form. This is illustrated in figure 6.6.

Figure 6.6 Sources of information

Source: Adapted from Cant et al. 2006. *Marketing management,* 5th ed. Cape Town: Juta, p 151.

The purpose of the MIS is to collect, analyse and evaluate all the information that is likely to be of value when making marketing and other decisions.[6] This means that the information system is situated between the marketers making decisions and the marketing environment. It is, in effect, the interface between the two. Note that it is not just marketing that makes use of the information. Production operations, research and development, and all the other functions in the business should have access to this information. The MIS will also help the company to attempt to identify possible change and reactions to it, as discussed in the previous section. Many companies have formal MIS structures, yet some small businesses do not have this but are very effective in using their informal channels to keep in touch with the dynamics of the market.

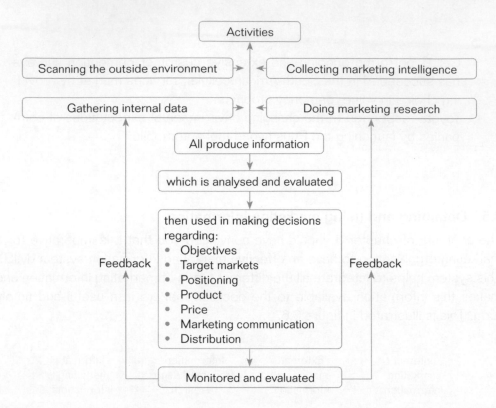

Figure 6.7 MIS and marketing decision making

Source: Adapted from Jobber, D. 2007. *Principles and practice of marketing*. London: McGraw-Hill, p 231.

Figure 6.7 shows the connection between the information received and marketing decisions. The figure indicates the firm's activities in terms of gathering data and information. Once this information has been analysed and evaluated, marketing management must respond to the information received by making key marketing decisions, as indicated. These changes or responses to the environment are then monitored and evaluated to determine whether the organisation is aligned to the environment and to the market, Remember, the value of information is in its use, so decisions must be made as to how to respond to meaningful change in the marketing environment. For example, Procter & Gamble often videotape the day-to-day behaviour of their consumers. By doing this with a sample of families in some European countries they found that the diaper itself was as important to new mothers as information and knowledge were. They responded by launching Pampers.com, which is an online community where mothers can obtain information on areas of concern for them.

6.6 Perspectives on consumer behaviour

One of the basic premises of marketing is that by understanding customers and their purchasing habits, marketers can design an effective offering to help them achieve their objectives.

There are many basic questions that any marketer must be able to answer about the market, such as who the customers are and why they buy. This information is invaluable because marketing is supposed to be the link between the customers and the organisation. Figure 6.8 illustrates the relationship between the environment, the marketer and the customer.

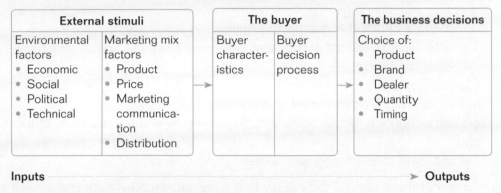

Figure 6.8 A simple model of buyer behaviour

Source: Adapted from Rix, P. 2004. *Marketing: A practical approach*. North Ryde: McGraw-Hill, p 141.

You will notice from figure 6.8 that the environmental variables under which all market players operate have an influence on the customer, as should the marketing mix designed by the marketer. These two aspects are *external stimuli* to the customer. There are also *internal stimuli* which affect the decisions made by the customer. Buyers' own characteristics, for example, will effect their decisions. Different customers will have different perceptions and expectations, and the manner in which buyers proceed through the decision-making process will also affect their decision. No two customers are exactly alike, and each one will have different individual or group influences. The involvement of buyers with the product will help to determine how seriously and systematically they proceed through the steps in the decision-making process. Lastly, buyers will make a number of decisions. The marketer's job, through the marketing mix, is to persuade them to buy the organisation's products and to deliver the need satisfaction to ensure that they remain loyal to the organisation.

As previously mentioned, the marketing environment is constantly changing, and thus must be monitored in order for the business to respond to changes in the marketing environment. Likewise, customers are also affected by changes in the environment, and their needs will also change. Any business, in order to be successful, must be aware of changing characteristics and needs of its customer base. These could be significant changes, which the business will have to address through its marketing activities.

Wilson and Gilligan in the late 1990s[7] identified a number of characteristics which are associated with what they term the 'new' consumer, which are:

- the development of new value systems;
- greater emphasis on value for money;
- higher levels of price awareness and price sensitivity;
- an increased demand for and a willingness to accept more and exciting new products;
- less fear of technology;
- lower levels of brand and supplier loyalty;
- a greater willingness to experiment with new products, ideas and delivery systems;
- a greater cynicism;
- higher levels of environmental awareness;
- greater scepticism about politicians, big business and traditional institutions; and
- the changing roles of men and women.

How many of these do you think apply to the current situation with consumers in South Africa? The connection of these characteristics with the marketing mix is self-evident.

The core of any marketing strategy is a commitment to understanding customer needs and problems. Figure 6.9 depicts this customer analysis.

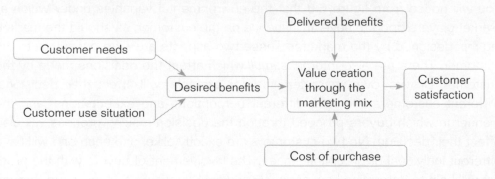

Figure 6.9 Customer analysis and the marketing mix

Source: Adapted from Walters, D & Lancaster G. 38/3. 2000. Implementing value strategy through the value chain. *Management Decision*, pp 160–178.

In figure 6.9, we see that a business must monitor the changing customer needs and the changing ways in which the customer uses the product. These two factors will affect the benefits which the customer is seeking and which the customer desires. The business responds to these through changes in some aspect of the marketing mix. By successfully meeting these customer needs and delivering the benefits desired, the business can satisfy its customers, increasing the likelihood of success. Note that the customers determine what value they receive from a business by considering the benefits which they perceive as being delivered to them against the cost of the product or service. This emphasises the importance of marketing management ensuring that its customers perceive that they are receiving value for money relative to what they would receive from competitors. In a previous example above we discussed Procter & Gamble and its research – where it was found that new mothers were more concerned about information than with diapers, so the company responded to this in order to retain customers and add value in areas of importance to them.

6.7 Target market selection and positioning

The importance of target market selection and positioning is best understood in terms of the phenomenon of *fragmentation*,[8] whereby technology and cultural differences contribute to the splintering of the market into diverse groups. This fragmentation is driven by differences in income, lifestyle, race and experiences. It means that markets are becoming smaller, and there will be a larger range of products and brands to cater to the differences among these markets. These are environmental aspects, many of which work together. In selecting a target market, marketers need to understand how to recognise the various groups which make up the total market. This process relies on marketing research which assists the marketer to find the best way to segment the market.

After the different segments have been identified, the market potential of each one must be established. Again, market research is instrumental in the selection of segments that will help the company to achieve its objectives.

Having decided on a specific target market (or markets), the marketer will have to determine how to position the product. In order to do this, further market research in terms of the competitor positions and need satisfaction may be required. Chapter 5 discussed the different options for positioning a product. Once the positioning strategy has been established, the marketing mix must be tailored to meet customer needs effectively. The marketing mix, if correctly designed, is the method by which the marketer meets the needs of the customers in such a way that the customer's perception of the product matches the positioning strategy selected by the marketer.

Note that there are continuous changes in the market, so the environment must be monitored continuously to determine whether repositioning is needed or not. Figure 6.10 shows the progression in terms of segmenting, targeting, positioning and designing the marketing mix. Let us now consider the marketing mix itself.

Figure 6.10 Progression for pinpointing the market

Source: Adapted from Groucutt, J, Leadley, P & Forsyth, P. 2004. *Marketing: Essential principles, new realities.* London: Kogan Page, p 129.

6.8 The marketing mix

The previous seven sections of this chapter formed the basis for this book. These are the building blocks upon which an effective marketing campaign is based. The care and attention to detail exercised by marketers with these building blocks will help them in terms of the key decision-making areas of marketing. These areas are the choice of a target market (or markets) and the design of an appropriate marketing mix for the chosen target market/s. The choice of a target market and positioning of the product offering in it market were dealt with in chapter 5 and briefly in section 6.7.

The second key decision-making area is the marketing mix. Although it is not the aim of this book to discuss the marketing mix in detail, we do need to introduce what the marketing mix is and briefly discuss the impact of these building blocks on the components of the marketing mix.

The marketing mix is a combination of marketing decisions designed to influence customers to buy the enterprise's products and/or services.[9] A more common term used to describe this mix is the *four Ps* of marketing: product, promotion, place and price. The *product* aspect of the marketing mix tries to ensure that the product characteristics match the benefits sought by the target customers. The *promotion* element tries to communicate the enterprise's ability to satisfy the customer through the use of communication such as advertising, personal selling, sales promotions and publicity. The *place* or distribution component of the marketing mix tries to deliver the right product to the right place at the right time to satisfy customer needs. Lastly, the *price* component of the mix tries to match the money that customers will pay for the product with the value customers receive through the purchase and use of the product. These four components work together to help the enterprise to achieve its marketing objectives, as shown in figure 6.11 and briefly discussed below.

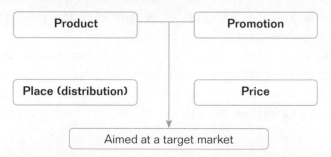

Figure 6.11 The four Ps of marketing

Source: Adapted from Jobber, D. 2008. *Principles and practice of marketing*, 5th ed. London: McGraw-Hill, p 22.

6.8.1 *Product decisions*

Product decisions are critical. The marketer must determine what the actual product offers, as well as the need-satisfying benefits which should be included.

The marketer needs to make decisions regarding the range of different types of products and/or services to make and offer. This is called the *product mix*.

Specific product strategies must be established: whether the product mix will be extended through product diversification; whether it will be reduced for more specialisation; whether to standardise the product range; how to differentiate or distinguish the product from other competitive products; and decisions on how to manage the possible obsolescence of the product. A plan for the development and commercialisation of the products must be developed. Both the product and package design are important, as they are so closely related to product decisions. The whole issue of a brand name and the branding decisions must be addressed, and plans made to establish brand awareness within the selected target markets.

Although product is usually the first component of the marketing mix addressed by marketing, the development and design of the product offering and package is totally dependent on the input from the environmental analysis and customer analyses. Without researching these two areas, the marketer cannot effectively design a product offering to meet the needs of the customer. For example, changing economic conditions may necessitate developing a lower-priced product item. Toyota SA developed the Tazz range of cars as a response to economic changes in the marketplace that generated more attention on entry-level car offerings. (The Tazz was eventually replaced by the Yaris range.)

Evolving use of products may necessitate packaging design changes. Both of these could lead to new product opportunities and/or brand extensions.

6.8.2 Pricing decisions

Price is important because it is the only element in the marketing mix that generates the revenue. It is also important because it affects the enterprise in a direct way, namely the profitability of the business. The marketer will need to establish the price sensitivity of the target customers, and will then need to establish the basic price. This can be done on the basis of costs, on the basis of the demand for a product, or on the basis of competitive pricing structures. All three of these factors will influence the setting of a price. The marketer must also establish flexibility in the pricing structure through the use of adjustments. These factors could include different types of discounts and the geographic location of the customers.

We have referred to the effect of the environment on pricing by noting that economic conditions could lead a marketer to develop a lower-priced alternative. The marketer must monitor the environment to analyse the effect of the environmental factors on pricing. New developments in materials and processes can have significant impact on a business's bottom line as a result of its impact in pricing and margins. Technology in particular has provided significant threats to many businesses by its accelerating rate of change, yet it also provides opportunities to improve bottom-line performance by improving profitability. Developments such as 'just-in-time', materials management systems and e-commerce have had a significant impact on the profit margins of motor vehicle manufacturers. Many cars are now sold through the Internet, with significant impact on promotion and distribution costs and therefore on pricing.

Marketers must also carefully research and monitor the target market's sensitivity to its pricing strategy. In India, shampoo manufacturers discovered that many lower-income consumers could not afford their shampoo offerings because the price was too high for the quantity offered. They responded by developing single-occasion sachets that allowed the consumer one shampoo, and priced it accordingly. This resulted in significant volume increase in amount of shampoo sold and on profitability.

Telecommunications industry drives prices down in South Africa

The granting of the third licence to Cell C to market cellular phone services in South Africa has led all the players in the industry to carefully consider their pricing strategies. A plethora of packages for the start-up user have been developed and there has been much more variation in terms of the possible renewal packages that a cellular phone user can purchase. As a result of technological innovation and increased competition in the industry, the number of options and prices has increased tremendously, benefiting the consumer through better value, increased costs and easier access for those customers who may not have as high a disposable income as others.

6.8.3 Distribution decisions

The marketer will have to establish the intensity of distribution needed to meet the market's needs and expectations. This could be *intensive, selective* or *exclusive* distribution intensity. The marketer will also have to decide on the type of distribution channel through which to deliver the product/service to the final consumers. There are many options to consider here, from direct channels through to those that utilise intermediaries such as retailers, wholesalers and agents. The effect of the physical position of the marketer's own business could be included here, as the location of a business is often the most critical determinant of possible success.

Distribution decisions and distribution channel design are two of the areas where rapid changes are occurring in terms of the marketing mix. The use of the Internet for direct sales is revolutionising the way many firms reach their customers. Dell overtook Compaq as the leading personal computer seller in the US, and one aspect that may have helped is that Dell had a completely different distribution strategy to Compaq. While Compaq distributed through the traditional computer retailer channels, Dell used a direct channel by selling to customers by means of the Internet. This innovation led to significant reductions in distribution costs and also had a direct effect on its pricing policy. It is critical for marketers to monitor both changes in the environment and customer expectations of where they want to purchase products. In so doing, they will always be able to meet customer needs by providing the right product at the right time.

6.8.4 Promotion decisions

It is essential for marketers to inform current and potential customers in the marketplace about their products and their marketing activities. This communication can be done by using marketing communication tools such as advertising, sales promotion, personal selling and publicity.

It is clear that there are a number of decisions associated with the use of these communication tools, such as what message to deliver, what media to use, what size budget is required, and what promotional support activities to implement. All of these must be applied, coordinated and evaluated. The marketer must also communicate internally throughout the organisation to ensure that the employees and staff are aware of what the expectations are in the marketplace and what message the organisation is delivering to its target audiences.

Media choices are an area to which marketers must pay particular attention. The growing number of media choices (Internet, intranet, hot-air balloons, travelling billboards, social networking sites like Facebook, new magazines and new television stations such as those accessed through satellite television) means that marketers have to pay particular attention to making the correct choices for communicating with the target markets in an effective manner. This requires systematic research of the customer base to monitor trends in terms of media as well as advertising-campaign impact. Nando's, for example, has been particularly effective in designing campaigns that are related in to current events in South Africa. Its success is as a result of monitoring the environment for opportunities.

'Taylor Made' and database marketing for golfers

Taylor Made is a well-known manufacturer and marketer of golf clubs and footwear, and its products are used by millions of golfers around the world. The leadership of Taylor Made, in terms of database marketing, has given them a significant advantage over their competitors in a very competitive industry. Their database consists of over 1,4 million names and addresses. This enables the company to contact and enhance relations with the users of its products. If individuals on the list, for example, have Internet access, they receive a weekly online magazine with information on golfing destinations and playing tips from golf professionals. In each mailing of the magazine, readers are asked information about products they prefer, prices, and so on. This is then used to input into product designs and pricing decisions. It can also merge its list with that of subscribers to golf magazines and then tailor e-mail ads to each category of subscriber.

Cause-related marketing provides opportunity for companies

Cause-related marketing is defined as any commercial activity by which business and charities or causes form a partnership with each other to market an image, product or service for mutual benefit. Many organisations are forming alliances with charities and causes so that they can develop win-win situations that benefit both parties. It must be mentioned that this implies a deeper relationship than just 'we give X rand for each amount spent with us'. It implies a collaboration where the business can help deliver tangible benefits to a relevant cause over a specified time period. A good example of this in South Africa is that of Nedcor and its 'Green Trust', which supports relevant environmental causes related to the physical environment and nature.

Source: Adapted from Barrett, D. 2002. *The rise of cause-related marketing.* Harvard Business School, Harvard College, p 2.

Harley-Davidson and the four Ps

Harley-Davidson provides a good example of how a company used the traditional four Ps of marketing to position its motorcycles to a new customer segment,[10] the baby boomer generation in the US. The product was changed by introducing a new engine, but the heavy-metal look was retained. The promotional strategy was changed by shifting the advertising to promote a softer image. It featured celebrities on a Harley-Davidson, the objective being to attract the high-income segment. It changed its distribution strategy by cleaning up the dealerships so that they did not look so dark and so that they were more customer friendly. Harley-Davidson does not sell only motorcycles now – it also sells motorcycle fashion accessories, which are displayed in a clean, bright atmosphere. The motorcycles are priced to reflect the value that the high-income earners place on living out their fantasies on a Harley-Davidson motorcycle. The upper end of the motorcycle range often runs into the $20 000 price range. All these components demonstrate a well-coordinated marketing mix targeted to a specific segment of the market.

Summary

In this chapter, we have established how the topics covered in the previous five chapters help to shape the decisions made by marketers in terms of the marketing mix. In fact, a number of analyses were needed in order to accomplish this. Firstly, the marketing orientation of the business was analysed to ensure that the company culture is correct and proactive. Secondly, the marketing environment and its effect on all the decision-making areas of marketing were highlighted. Thirdly, we emphasised the importance of marketing research in order to align the market offering with the marketing environment and to meet customer needs. This all entails a thorough understanding of the customer and the characteristics that affect the decisions made in terms of purchasing. Lastly, target market selection and positioning is critical, as all the decisions made by marketing are as a result of selection and positioning, which are the main consideration for all marketing decisions. Figure 6.12 places the philosophy and approach discussed in this book into context.

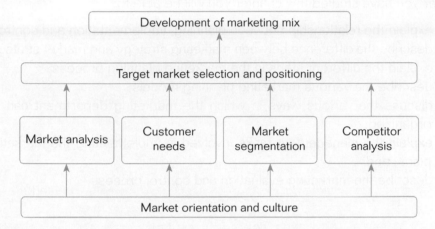

Figure 6.12 Core analysis for marketing decisions

References

1. Cant, MC, Strydom, JW, Jooste, CJ & Du Plessis, PJ. 2006. *Marketing management,* 5th ed. Cape Town: Juta, pp 19–22.
2. Dibb, S & Simkin, L. 2008. *Marketing planning: A workbook for marketing managers.* London: Cenage Learning, pp 94–105.
3. Adapted from Cant et al, op cit, pp 10–15.
4. Ibid, pp 10–11.
5. Cant et al, op cit, pp 34–36.
6. Rix, P. 2004. *Marketing: A practical approach.* North Ryde: McGraw-Hill, p 64.
7. Wilson, RMS & Gilligan, C. 1997. *Strategic marketing management.* Oxford: Butterworth-Heinemann, p 158.
8. Jobber, D. 2008. *Principles and practice of marketing,* 5th ed. London: McGraw-Hill, p 547.
9. Ibid, p 56.
10. Adapted from Assael, H. 1998. *Marketing.* Orlando: The Dryden Press, pp 18–19.

CHAPTER SEVEN

Marketing planning, implementation and control

Learning objectives

After you have studied this chapter you will be able to:

* explain the relationship between planning, implementation and control;
* describe the difference between marketing strategy and market strategy;
* explain the different steps in the marketing planning process;
* describe the various marketing planning models;
* discuss the various ways in which the marketing department can be organised;
* explain the management tasks involved in implementing the marketing plans; and
* describe the marketing evaluation and control process.

7.1   Introduction

In the first six chapters of this book we highlighted a number of important issues the marketing manager must focus on. We have not discussed the components of a marketing strategy in detail but referred to it in chapter 6, where we discussed the integration of all the components of marketing. In order for any strategy to be successful, however, it is essential that the total marketing process be managed. This by implication means that the decisions made must be implemented, monitored and evaluated, and corrective action taken if needed.

The process of planning, implementation and control is the responsibility of marketing management and must be conducted on a continuous basis. It is not sufficient to do this only once a year or term. It makes no sense to spend vast amounts of money and time on planning the marketing strategy of selected segments and not implementing what has been decided. In the same way it does not make sense to implement a plan without monitoring it to see if the outcomes are met. These actions refer to the planning, implementation and control of marketing actions. Imagine all the planning that goes into the launching of a new washing powder aimed at housewives. To implement it, responsibilities must be allocated, time frames indicated and launch dates set, etc. After the product has been launched, it must be established whether sales were as expected, whether

they were by the intended target market, what repeat purc
targets were met.

This chapter is based on figure 7.1, which shows the rela
three main management functions of the marketing departm

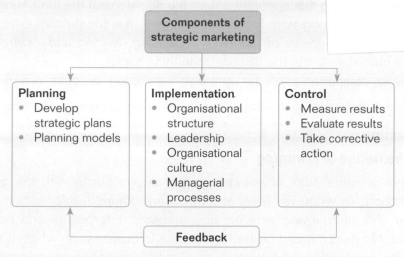

Figure 7.1 The relationship between planning, implementation and control

Source: Adapted from Cant, MC, Strydom, JW, Jooste, CJ & Du Plessis. 2006. *Marketing management,* 5th ed. Cape Town: Juta, p 545.

7.1 Strategic marketing management

7.1.1 The meaning of strategic marketing management

The process of strategic marketing management involves in essence three steps, which are:

- step 1 – planning;
- step 2 – implementation; and
- step 3 – evaluation.

A close relationship exists between these steps, which is clearly depicted in figure 7.2.[2]

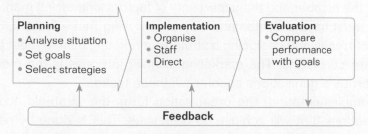

Figure 7.2 The marketing management process

Source: Rix, P. 2004. *Marketing: A practical approach,* 5th ed. Australia: McGraw-Hill.

...arketing management implies that the above process takes place in a ...context; in other words, with a long-term view towards achieving organi-...al goals, and integrating marketing goals and objectives with the overall ...als and objectives of the organisation.

Strategic marketing management entails the decisions of the marketing department with a view to long-term growth and survival in a competitive environment. All the management tasks of *planning*, *organising*, *leading* and *controlling* are taken into consideration in the discussion in this chapter.

The three components of the strategic marketing process are discussed below.

7.2 Planning

7.2.1 *The nature of planning*

Planning is a central task of marketing, and always starts with the gathering of information. At whatever level strategies are planned, information is gathered from the internal and external environments, interpreted and constantly monitored. No decision can be better than the information on which it is based and therefore extensive marketing research and forecasting must first be done. Marketing managers must, for instance, do a detailed SWOT analysis to clearly indicate what can or cannot be done and where lucrative opportunities can be exploited.[3]

Planning has many advantages for any business. These advantages include:[4]

- encouraging systematic thinking about the future;
- leading to improved coordination between different departments and levels of management;
- establishing performance standards for measuring results;
- providing a logical basis for decision making;
- improving the organisation's ability to cope with change, and enabling it to succeed in a rapidly changing business environment, and
- enhancing the organisation's ability to identify marketing opportunities.

Because of the number and the uncertainty of factors influencing market success, a business must have a systematic way of analysing these factors, determining the impact of trends and designing a strategic marketing plan to meet present and future market conditions. The marketing planning process is the mechanism by which numerous organisations accomplish these tasks.

Through implementation, the organisation turns the strategic and marketing plans into actions that will achieve its objectives. This is done by people in the marketing organisation working with others, both inside and outside the business. In order to assess the success of the marketing plans, it is imperative that the results of these plans are measured and evaluated. If necessary, the results of this procedure must lead to corrective action to ensure that the objectives are reached. Marketing analysis provides information and evaluations needed for all the other marketing activities.

The fact that planning is being discussed first does not mean that it always comes first, or that planning ends before marketers move on to other activities. Figure 7.1 also shows that planning and the other activities are all dependent on the results of preceding analysis.

7.2.2 The marketing planning process

A marketing plan can broadly be described as a written document containing the guidelines for a business unit's marketing programmes and allocations over the planning period. Therefore, all relevant quantitative and qualitative details must be mentioned in the marketing plan, and they must also be very specific.[5]

The need for planning is now almost universally accepted by managers, even though it is not as widely implemented in practice. The use of marketing plans also delivers the following benefits.[6]

- *Consistency.* Marketing action plans will be consistent with the overall corporate plan as well as with the other functional plans.
- *Responsibility.* Those people responsible for implementing the individual parts of the marketing plan will know their responsibilities and their performance can be monitored against these.
- *Communication.* Those involved in implementing the plans will also know through effective communication what the overall objectives are, as well as the assumptions which lie behind them.
- *Commitment.* If all involved agree to the plans, their agreement should stimulate a group commitment.

Marketing planning is by its very nature a *future-directed activity*. Comprehensive and reliable information about all applicable environmental variables is necessary in order to make an educated estimate of what the future holds in store. Strategic decisions taken today may be implemented only at a much later stage. Marketing planning usually occurs in the *short*, *medium* and *long term*. In the short term (usually one year) it is reasonably easy to make forecasts. In the medium term (three to five years) it is more difficult, and long-term forecasts (five years and longer) are increasingly risky and uncertain. Nevertheless, all these planning phases are crucial for long-term survival and growth.

Scanning the environment is an important step in planning. In many instances a marketing audit will form the basis of this environmental scan. This can be a complex process, but the aim is simple – to identify those existing (external and internal) factors which will have a significant impact on the future plans of the organisation.

A technique which is particularly useful in the analysis of the material contained in the environmental scan is the SWOT (strengths, weaknesses, opportunities and threats) analysis. SWOT groups the key pieces of information into two main categories, namely *internal factors* and *external factors*.

Internal factors

Internal factors refer to the strengths and weaknesses within the organisation. The internal variables in respect of resources, abilities and skills are discussed elsewhere.

External factors

External factors refer to the opportunities and threats presented by the external environment. Information on these variables is systematised and kept up to date in a marketing information system, making it conveniently available for planning purposes and market forecasting.

A SWOT analysis can be described as a summary of the major findings of the organisation's current situation under the headings *strengths*, *weaknesses*, *opportunities* and *threats*, as illustrated in table 7.1.[7]

Table 7.1 The components of a SWOT analysis

Strengths	Weaknesses
This describes the activities that an organisation does well and that set it apart from competitors, e.g. a skilled labour force	These are the areas on which a company should improve if it does not want competitors to gain advantage, e.g. when a company does not have enough working capital
Opportunities	**Threats**
These consist of the situations that exist in the marketing environment that the organisation can exploit to its own benefit, e.g. when a new consumer need arises in the market that the company can fulfil	These are the situations that exist in the marketing environment which the organisation cannot exploit to its advantage, but that pose a threat to the profitability of the organisation, e.g. when a new innovative need-satisfying product is introduced by competitors that may make the organisation's product obsolete

Source: Adapted from Strydom, JW. 2004. *Introduction to marketing,* 3rd ed. Wetton: Juta.

7.3 Implementation

The second step in the strategic marketing management process is implementation – without it, planning is useless to any organisation. Strategy implementation is discussed as outlined in figure 7.3.[8]

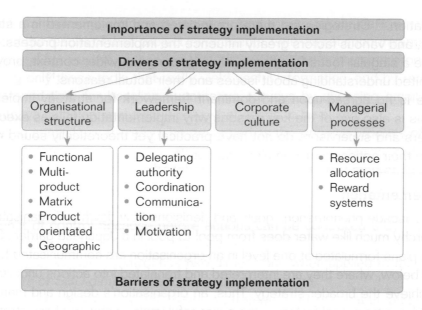

Figure 7.3 Important factors of strategy implementation

Source: Adapted from Cant, MC, Strydom, JW, Jooste, CJ & Du Plessis. 2006. *Marketing management,* 5th ed. Cape Town: Juta, p 566.

7.3.1 The importance of implementation

Implementation is one of the key routes to improved business performance, but is often recognised as one of the most difficult business challenges facing today's managers. Implementation is often recognised as one of the greatest Achilles heels for all strategy initiatives.[9] The organisation should therefore now shift its focus from *strategy formulation* to *strategy implementation.*[10]

Companies no longer underestimate the importance of strategic intent and therefore, in a sense, know what to do. Their difficulties now lie in how to achieve the necessary changes. More than 70% of companies fail to implement new strategic initiatives and, given the significance of this area, the focus of strategic management has now shifted from the formulation of strategy to the implementation thereof.[11]

Even the most well-designed market and marketing strategies can fail without effective organising and structure, and good leadership. The implementation of marketing plans depends to a large extent on the organisational structure and the close cooperation of all marketing personnel under the leadership of the marketing manager. Planning and organising are thus closely linked. Benoma describes the interrelationship between strategy and implementation in the following manner.

Implementation strategies refer to the overall approach or framework for implementation. More simply put, the implementation strategy refers to *what* the organisation is going to do. This differs from *activities*, as the latter refers to the details of *how* the organisation is going to do this. The use of the word *strategy* implies that it is the overall approach of the organisation towards implementation, which is linked to a wide time frame, as well as the overall strategy of the

It is imperative that an organisation has a systematic basis according to which marketing effort is evaluated and controlled at both corporate and product level. Figure 7.5 is a model of marketing evaluation and control.[23]

7.4.2 Steps in the evaluation and control process

We will now discuss each of the steps in the model.

Step 1: Establish performance criteria[24]

Standards, as achievable objectives, can be determined for various marketing activities and are especially useful with routine activities, such as the number of visits and demonstrations per day expected of sales representatives. Standards can naturally also be laid down for once-off marketing projects, for example activities involved in a specific advertising campaign.

Furthermore, standards can be set in quantitative and qualitative terms for the different marketing activities. Quantitative (or financial) standards are emphasised in this section, and consist of input, output and efficiency standards.

Step 2: Develop performance projections[25]

Once the company has established the criteria it will use to evaluate marketing performance, it develops performance projections for products and business units in the form of a profit-and-loss statement.

To develop a profit-and-loss statement, management must establish a budget for a product or SBU that will provide cost and revenue estimates. Today many companies are using a variation of an objective-task approach known as *zero-based budgeting* in which the budget is determined at the beginning of each year. Past sales or competitive expenditures are not considered. Instead, certain profitability goals are formulated, and management asks what actions are required to meet these goals, and then estimates the necessary expenditures.

Zero-based budgeting is popular as it provides a more objective basis for evaluating marketing performance. It simplifies evaluating product or SBU performance because expenditures are evaluated from a zero starting point. Many companies assess marketing expenditures by comparing them to expenditures in previous years. A company might say that a R5 million advertising budget for the year is 10% higher than the previous year and evaluate advertising results on this basis. The fallacy is that last year's budget might have been too high or too low to begin with. Zero-based budgeting overcomes this problem by assessing costs from a base of zero, so that if R5 million is spent on advertising this year, the basis for assessing the value of this expenditure is the profit it produces without reference to past expenditures.

Step 3: Develop a marketing organisation

This step requires establishing a marketing organisation capable of implementing and evaluating marketing strategies. The different marketing organisation structures have already been discussed.

Step 4: Develop the marketing plan

The development and implementation of a marketing plan has previously been widely discussed. It is, however, important to realise that *people* are involved in the implementation of plans, and that conflict and resistance can arise. A critical requirement is therefore a corporate culture conducive to harmony in the company.

Step 5: Evaluate marketing performance[26]

Evaluation takes place through comparing the *actual results* with the *formulated performance standards*. Managers therefore need to systematically investigate whether or not activities have been performed according to the performance standards set in the marketing plan.[27] Strategic control points are established and overseen by persons who have the required authority to exercise control. The product manager, the advertising manager and the sales manager, *inter alia*, are responsible for measuring and noting actual performance against the preset standards in their departments.

It has already been mentioned that evaluation is appropriate before the actual activity takes place, while it takes place, and after it has been completed. The ideal is to evaluate before or at least while things are happening so that deviations from the standard can be spotted in time and changes made before money or time is wasted. However, this is not always possible, and marketing control is often required after the event has occurred. Then it is a matter of *recovery management*. The purpose of recovery management is to establish a basis for future planning and to prevent a repetition of the deviation in future – this points to *preventive management*. In large organisations it is often difficult for management to exercise effective control. Strategic control points are thus delegated to the lower levels, while only exceptional differences and deviations from the standards are reported to top management. This is referred to as *control by exception*. Where deviations occur, the nature and extent thereof and the reasons therefore have to be determined before corrective steps can be taken.

Step 6: Take corrective action

Where actual performance is below the standards set, steps can be taken to improve performance. If sales in the first quarter are lower than the norm set in the sales budget, then corrective measures can possibly entail an intensive marketing campaign. Corrective action can be taken in three areas: *territory decisions*, *product decisions* and *customer and order-size decisions*. For example, if the relative profitability of each product or group of products is known, informed decisions can be taken. As in the case of unprofitable models, sizes or colours can be eliminated; salespeople's compensation plans may be altered to encourage the sale of high-margin items; or channels of distribution may be changed. Even though specific actions are possible in each area, there are three broad guidelines that can be followed in terms of decision making, as described below.

When significant discrepancies have been detected between *actual* performance and the *set* performance standards, it must be decided whether deviations warrant correction. These deviations can be dealt with accordingly by:

- taking corrective action that eliminates the cause of the deviation;
- changing performance standards if it becomes clear that the standards set in the marketing plan are no longer realistic; or
- keeping the same goals and allowing the deviation from the plan to continue.

Where the deviation can be attributed to uncontrollable environmental factors (such as an economic depression), standards have to be lowered if they were initially set too high. In favourable circumstances it is also possible that actual performance can exceed the standards laid down. Once again, standards will have to be adjusted. If sales in the first quarter are much higher than the norm set in the sales budget, an adjustment will have to be made to avoid stock problems in the second quarter.

Information on deviations, the reasons for deviations and the nature of corrective action are used in the forecasting process in order to set more accurate standards for future periods.

Summary

The three components of strategic marketing, namely *planning*, *implementation* and *control*, direct the marketing task in the organisation. Marketing and market strategies are planned by marketing management, taking the internal strengths and weaknesses as well as the external opportunities and threats into consideration. The strategies are market driven, and consumer needs, demands and preferences, and the competitive position of the organisation are considered. The main objective of the organisation, namely maximisation of profitability, can be realised only through aggressive marketing efforts, the creation of an effective organisational structure, the judicious application of resources and the establishment of an evaluation system through which performance standards are set and activities controlled.

References

1. Cant, MC, Strydom, JW, Jooste, CJ & Du Plessis, PJ. 2006. *Marketing management,* 5th ed. Cape Town: Juta, p 545.
2. Rix, P. 2004. *Marketing: A practical approach,* 5th ed. Australia: McGraw-Hill, p 421.
3. Strydom, JW. 2004. *Introduction to marketing,* 3rd ed. Wetton: Juta.

4. Ibid.

5. Ibid.

6. Mercer, D in Cant, MC et al. 2006. *Marketing management*, 5th ed. Cape Town: Juta, p 549.

7. Strydom, JW. 2004. *Introduction to marketing*, 3rd ed. Wetton: Juta.

8. Cant, MC et al, op cit, p 566.

9. Meldrum, M & Atkinson, S in Cant, MC et al. 2006. *Marketing management*, 5th ed. Cape Town: Juta, p 549.

10. Pearce, JA & Robinson, RB. 2005. *Strategic management: Formulation, implementation and control*, 9th ed. New York: McGraw-Hill Irwin.

11. Bartlett, CA in Okumus, F. 2003. Framework to implement strategies in organisations. *Management Decision*, 41(9). [Online] Available from: Proquest: ABI/Inform Global: http://proquest.umi.com/login (accessed: 5 August 2005).

12. Steyn, B & Puth, G. 2000. *Corporate communication strategy.* Cape Town: Heinemann.

13. Okumus, F. 2003. Framework to implement strategies in organisations. *Management Decision*, 41(9). [Online] Available from: Proquest: ABI/Inform Global: http://proquest.umi.com/login (accessed: 5 August 2005).

14. Ibid.

15. Ibid.

16. Swanepoel, H. 1996. *Community development: Putting plans in action.* Wetton: Juta.

17. Steyn, B & Nunes, M. 2001. Communication strategy for community development: A case study of the Heifer project – South Africa. *Communicatio*, 27(2): 29–48.

18. Crawford, P & Bryce, P. 2003. Project monitoring and evaluation: A method for enhancing the efficiency and effectiveness of aid project implementation. *International Journal of Project Management*, 21: 363–373.

19. Coldevin, G. 2001. *Participatory communication and adult learning for rural development.* Food and Agricultural Organisation of the United Nations: FAO.

20. Assael, H in Cant, MC et al. 2006. *Marketing management*, 5th ed. Cape Town: Juta.

21. Assael, op cit, pp 644–645.

22. Crawford & Bryce, op cit, p 584.

23. Van der Walt, A, Strydom, WJ, Marx, S & Jooste, CJ in Cant, MC et al. 2006. *Marketing management*, 5th ed. Cape Town: Juta, p 583.

24. Van der Walt et al in Cant, MC et al. 2006. *Marketing management*, 5th ed. Cape Town: Juta, p 584.

25. Assael, op cit, p 650.

26. Van der Walt et al in Cant, MC et al. 2006. *Marketing management*, 5th ed. Cape Town: Juta.

27. Strydom, op cit.

Index

Entries are listed in letter-by-letter alphabetical order. Page references in *italic* indicate where you can find a figure or table relating to the index entry term.